Economic Issues, Problems and Perspectives

Macroeconomics

Principles, Applications and Challenges

ECONOMIC ISSUES, PROBLEMS AND PERSPECTIVES

Additional books in this series can be found on Nova's website under the Series tab.

Additional e-books in this series can be found on Nova's website under the e-book tab.

ECONOMIC ISSUES, PROBLEMS AND PERSPECTIVES

MACROECONOMICS

PRINCIPLES, APPLICATIONS AND CHALLENGES

CARLY M. HUTSON
EDITOR

New York

NOTICE TO THE READER

The Publisher has taken reasonable care in the preparation of this book, but makes no expressed or implied warranty of any kind and assumes no responsibility for any errors or omissions. No liability is assumed for incidental or consequential damages in connection with or arising out of information contained in this book. The Publisher shall not be liable for any special, consequential, or exemplary damages resulting, in whole or in part, from the readers' use of, or reliance upon, this material. Any parts of this book based on government reports are so indicated and copyright is claimed for those parts to the extent applicable to compilations of such works.

Independent verification should be sought for any data, advice or recommendations contained in this book. In addition, no responsibility is assumed by the publisher for any injury and/or damage to persons or property arising from any methods, products, instructions, ideas or otherwise contained in this publication.

This publication is designed to provide accurate and authoritative information with regard to the subject matter covered herein. It is sold with the clear understanding that the Publisher is not engaged in rendering legal or any other professional services. If legal or any other expert assistance is required, the services of a competent person should be sought. FROM A DECLARATION OF PARTICIPANTS JOINTLY ADOPTED BY A COMMITTEE OF THE AMERICAN BAR ASSOCIATION AND A COMMITTEE OF PUBLISHERS.

Additional color graphics may be available in the e-book version of this book.

Library of Congress Cataloging-in-Publication Data

Macroeconomics : principles, applications and challenges / editor, Carly M. Hutson.
pages cm. -- (Economic issues, problems and perspectives)
Includes index.
ISBN 978-1-63463-596-7 (softcover)
1. Macroeconomics. I. Hutson, Carly M.
HB172.5.M3362 2014
339--dc23 2014044412

Published by Nova Science Publishers, Inc. † New York

CONTENTS

PREFACE

The first chapter in this book deals with an analysis of determinants of both net international investment positions and net costs of negative investment positions in transitive countries. It defines sustainable conditions that assume foreign investors will be prepared to continue to (re)finance negative investment positions in short and long-time periods. The sustainability conditions are derived from dynamics of both sources created through net export surplus and negative net yields paid from an international investment position. This chapter points out important differences between a position of large advanced and small transitive economies in the case of net costs of a negative net investment position. The second chapter examines the Messe-Rogoff puzzle, which demonstrates that exchange rate models cannot outperform the random walk in out-of-sample forecasting. The final chapter assesses the productivity change and efficiency of banks in Ghana.

Chapter 1 – This chapter deals with an analysis of determinants of both net international investment position and net costs of negative investment position in transitive countries. It defines a sustainability conditions that assume foreign investors will be prepared to continue to (re)finance negative investment position in short and long time period. The sustainability conditions are derived from dynamics of both sources created through net export surplus and negative net yields paid from international investment position. The chapter points out important differences between a position of large advanced and small transitive economies in case of net costs of negative net investment position. It is discussed in detail that the dynamic of net yields is based on factors like country's position of FDI lender/debtor, country's currency position of world investment/invoicing currency, exogeneity of foreign asset's and liability's interest yields, role of FX reserves accumulation by country's central bank and last but not least position of foreign currency denominated loans on foreign liabilities. Transitive countries are prone to pay high net costs of negative investments position due to less favorable characteristics comparing with large advanced countries. The empirical analysis on an example of the Czech Republic in 1999-2011 demonstrates high levels of costs paid from the negative international investment position (particularly on the side of dividend and interest yields) that exceed the resources that domestic economy generates within net export surplus and balance of transfers and returns on labor. Besides, the Czech economy is not able to fulfil the condition of sustainability in the long run and mostly not even in the short run. It is to note that the long-term trends of particular variables in the condition of sustainability show quite different characteristics in comparison with mutual relations in the short run. These relations mostly confirm a number of positive trends, e.g. an increase in the economy's capacity to generate resources in the situation of an increase in the costs paid from international investments position, anti-cyclic behavior of international investment position to GDP ratio in relation to foreign demand and endogeneity of the interest yield of foreign liabilities. On the contrary, it is clearly confirmed that the worsening ratio of international investment position to GDP is a result of high dividend costs paid from foreign property liabilities, the first differences of which are negatively related to a change in foreign demand for domestic export, and last but not least, the strong counteractive reaction of CZK/EUR exchange rate appears as significant if a change in the economic growth rate occurs.

Chapter 2 – The Messe-Rogoff puzzle has been a debatable topic since 1983 when Richard Meese and Kenneth Rogoff demonstrated that no exchange rate model can outperform the random walk in out-of-sample forecasting. This finding been taken to imply the weakness of international economics and finance and raised the question as to why firms spend money on exchange rate forecasts and use them as an input in the financial decision making process when these forecasts are inferior to those of the random walk. In this chapter the authors resolve the puzzle by reaching the following conclusions: (i) we should expect nothing but that exchange rate models cannot outperform the random walk in out-of-sample forecasting if forecasting accuracy is measured by metrics that depend on the magnitude of the forecasting error only; (ii) the use of dynamic models to outperform the random walk is inappropriate because it is tantamount to beating a random walk with a random walk; and (iii) it is possible to outperform the random walk in terms of other metrics such as direction accuracy and profitability.

Chapter 3 – This study assesses total factor productivity growth (and its components, such as technical efficiency change, technical change, pure technical efficiency change, scale efficiency change) and technical efficiency (and its components, such pure technical efficiency and scale efficiency) in Ghana's banking industry for the period 2002-2010, sub-periods 2002-2006 and 2007-2010 as a result of Ghana's bank deregulation. This paper employs the data envelopment analysis (DEA) method and DEA-based Malmquist total factor productivity index to measure and decompose the overall technical efficiency and total factor productivity growth, respectively. The results suggest that Ghana's banks are technical inefficiency for the period 2002-2010 as well as the sub-periods, which is attributed to both pure technical and scale inefficiency. In addition, the results show total factor productivity grew on average over the period 2002-2010 and sub-period 2002-2006. The improvements in both periods are exclusively driven by technological progress because of deterioration in efficiency change for both periods. However, the findings exhibit the deterioration in total factor productivity for the period 2007-2010 is exclusively the result of the decline in efficiency change. All three periods report a decline in efficiency change due to the deterioration in both pure technical and scale efficiency change. The most remarkable years are 2005/2006 and 2007/2008 where the total factor productivity and its components all improved.

In: Macroeconomics
Editor: Carly M. Hutson

ISBN: 978-1-63463-596-7

Chapter 1

SUSTAINABILITY OF NEGATIVE INTERNATIONAL INVESTMENT POSITION IN TRANSITIVE COUNTRIES: THE CASE OF THE CZECH REPUBLIC IN 2000-2011[1]

Karel Brůna*
University of Economics in Prague, Czech Republic

ABSTRACT

This chapter deals with an analysis of determinants of both net international investment position and net costs of negative investment position in transitive countries. It defines a sustainability conditions that assume foreign investors will be prepared to continue to (re)finance negative investment position in short and long time period. The sustainability conditions are derived from dynamics of both sources created through net export surplus and negative net yields paid from international investment position. The chapter points out important differences between a position of large advanced and small transitive economies in case of net costs of negative net investment position. It is discussed in detail that the dynamic of net yields is based on factors like

[1] This chapter is processed as an output of a research project IP100040 supported by University of Economics in Prague, Faculty of Finance and Accounting.

* E-Mail: Bruna@Vse.Cz.

country's position of FDI lender/debtor, country's currency position of world investment/invoicing currency, exogeneity of foreign asset's and liability's interest yields, role of FX reserves accumulation by country's central bank and last but not least position of foreign currency denominated loans on foreign liabilities. Transitive countries are prone to pay high net costs of negative investments position due to less favorable characteristics comparing with large advanced countries.

The empirical analysis on an example of the Czech Republic in 1999-2011 demonstrates high levels of costs paid from the negative international investment position (particularly on the side of dividend and interest yields) that exceed the resources that domestic economy generates within net export surplus and balance of transfers and returns on labor. Besides, the Czech economy is not able to fulfil the condition of sustainability in the long run and mostly not even in the short run. It is to note that the long-term trends of particular variables in the condition of sustainability show quite different characteristics in comparison with mutual relations in the short run. These relations mostly confirm a number of positive trends, e.g. an increase in the economy's capacity to generate resources in the situation of an increase in the costs paid from international investments position, anti-cyclic behavior of international investment position to GDP ratio in relation to foreign demand and endogeneity of the interest yield of foreign liabilities. On the contrary, it is clearly confirmed that the worsening ratio of international investment position to GDP is a result of high dividend costs paid from foreign property liabilities, the first differences of which are negatively related to a change in foreign demand for domestic export, and last but not least, the strong counteractive reaction of CZK/EUR exchange rate appears as significant if a change in the economic growth rate occurs.

INTRODUCTION

Current debates of economists are dominated by problems connected with debt crisis in many advanced countries. The issues are high fiscal deficits and hardly sustainable indebtedness of the public sector while such parameters are discussed that would enable to improve the existing position of particular economies. However, the debt crisis is in many times accompanied by problems with external imbalance resulting from high current account deficits and worsening net foreign assets/net international investment position (NFA) of a country. Traditionally, the dynamics of net export of goods and services is considered highly significant in these debates. But the factors behind net costs the economies have to pay as the price of negative NFA are analyzed to a much lesser extent.

In the framework of debt problems of the Eurozone countries these problems are naturally overshadowed because based on the monetary union definition the exchange rate of the euro cannot counterbalance the problems of particular economies. But it does not imply that the economies do not have to shoulder the costs of negative NFA and that in the absence of the exchange rate adjustment process these costs are not reflected in other parts of the economic system. An example may be the significant negative position of central banks in PIGS countries towards ECB (in their TARGET 2 accounts) due to the net outflow of funds because of the current account deficit financed by supply of new liquidity to the banking sector of PIGS countries through ECB main refinancing operations.

The present chapter contains a theoretical analysis of factors behind the costs of negative NFA. In Part I the formal framework of the analysis is created focused on the dynamics of NFA in relation to GDP and factors influencing the cost of negative NFA. Part II contains a definition of condition to sustainability of NFA in short and long run. Part III describes a somewhat paradoxical case when the negative NFA of the USA is connected with net positive yields. Causes of this unusual phenomenon are interpreted in detail. A discussion is also focused on to what extent such a situation is possible in transition economies and on the factors causing that transition economies usually tend to pay relatively high costs of negative NFA, which ultimately may threat its sustainability. Part IV contains an empirical analysis of factors behind growing negative NFA in the Czech Republic and an econometric test of determinants of net costs of negative NFA in the period of 1999-2011.

I. Basic Factors of the Dynamics of Country's Net Foreign Assets in Relation to Gross Domestic Product

The NFA_T of a country expressed in domestic currency is defined as a difference between the value of foreign assets of residents of a given country in domestic currency (FA_T) and the value of foreign liabilities of residents in domestic currency (FL_T) in residents' balances at a certain point in time T. Foreign assets can be understood as a specific portfolio composed of foreign direct investments, portfolio investments, derivatives, other investments of residents toward non-residents and foreign exchange reserves of the central bank of a given country. Foreign liabilities are an otherwise structured portfolio consisting of non-residents' receivables toward residents by virtue of foreign direct investments, portfolio investments, derivatives and other investments. NFA at the actual point in time is derived from NFA at the end of the previous period (NFA_{T-1}) and operations influencing residents' foreign assets and liabilities over a certain period due to fluxes of capital connected with financing the balance of net export (NX_t), balance of labor income (L_t) and balance of current and capital transfers (TR_t) and in the form of net interest and dividend yields/costs from foreign assets and liabilities, the balance of retained profits and net changes in market value of foreign assets and liabilities resulting from net capital and exchange rate profits/losses:

$$\mathrm{NFA_T} = \mathrm{NFA_{T-1}} + \mathrm{NX_t} + \mathrm{TR_t} + \left[\mathrm{ir_t} + \mathrm{div_t} + \mathrm{rp_t} + \mathrm{cg_t} + \mathrm{er_t}(1 + \mathrm{ir_t} + \mathrm{div_t} + \mathrm{cg_t} + \mathrm{rp_t})\right]\mathrm{NFA_{T-1}} \quad (1)$$

where $ir_t{+}er_t ir_t$ expresses the average rate of return on NFA resulting from interest payout from debt assets and liabilities, $div_t{+}er_t div_t$ is the average rate of return on NFA resulting from dividend payout from property assets and liabilities, $rp_t{+}er_t rp_t$ is the average rate of retained profits from NFA, $cg_t{+}er_t cg_t$ is the average rate of capital profits/losses from NFA derived from changes in market prices of foreign assets/liabilities and er_t is the level of exchange rate profits/losses from NFA reflecting the relative change in the nominal effective exchange rate of domestic currency in relation to foreign currencies composing the portfolio of foreign assets and liabilities. All the rates of return are calculated on a basis of changes in home currency value of specific type of yield.

Equation (1) is a modification of the formula used in Miles-Feretti (2002), who did not explicitly distinguish between interest and dividend yield, rate of retained profits and did not work with the effect of exchange rate profits/losses resulting from the NFA of a country. In equation (1) the term $(ir_t + div_t + rp_t + cg_t)$ expresses total percentage yields/costs of NFA excluding the influence of exchange rate changes. The term $er_t(1 + ir_t + div_t + rp_t + cg_t)$ expresses the percentage value of exchange rate profits/losses resulting from both the NFA and realized net yields/costs related to this NFA. Total costs/yields the economy pays/gains from NFA represent costs/yields expressed by the formula $\alpha_t = ir_t + div_t + rp_t + cg_t + er_t(1 + ir_t + div_t + cg_t + rp_t)$. Within the costs/yields from NFA it is possible to distinguish costs/yields that are connected with net cash flow between residents and non-residents $(ir_t + div_t + er_t(ir_t + div_t))$, and costs/yields resulting from retained profits and from market value changes $(rp_t + cg_t + er_t(1 + rp_t + cg_t))$, which do not cause any cash flow in the actual period but may be connected with cash flow in future periods.

A crucial status criterion of external balance sustainability is the relation between the actual level of NFA and nominal gross domestic product (GDP). *Per se*, it is a very rough criterion omitting a number of structural factors that also determine sustainability of the existing situation in economy. They include e.g. evident differences in the size of this criterion between small open and large closed economies, the influence of different structure of foreign assets and liabilities as the relations between direct foreign investments and short-term debt capital, differences in the ratio of foreign indebtedness of the public and private sector, etc. In spite of these limitations the long-term dynamics of NFA/GDP ratio has become a closely watched variable that is used for the evaluation of sustainability of external trade and financial relations of an economy or as the basic indicator of imminent currency crisis. Based on rearrangement of equation (1) NFA in relation to actual GDP can be expressed as follows:

$$\frac{\mathrm{NFA_T}}{\mathrm{GDP_t}} = \frac{\mathrm{NX_t}}{\mathrm{GDP_t}} + \frac{\mathrm{TR_t}}{\mathrm{GDP_t}} + \frac{1+\mathrm{ir_t} + \mathrm{div_t} + \mathrm{rp_t} + \mathrm{cg_t} + \mathrm{er_t}(1 + \mathrm{ir_t} + \mathrm{div_t} + \mathrm{rp_t} + \mathrm{cg_t})}{1+\gamma_t}$$
$$\cdot\frac{\mathrm{NFA_{T-1}}}{\mathrm{GDP_{t-1}}} = = \frac{\mathrm{NX_t}}{\mathrm{GDP_t}} + \frac{\mathrm{TR_t}}{\mathrm{GDP_t}} + \frac{1+\alpha_t}{1+\gamma_t}\cdot\frac{\mathrm{NFA_{T-1}}}{\mathrm{GDP_{t-1}}} \tag{2}$$

where γ_t expresses the actual growth rate of GDP. Formula (2) shows that the maintenance of external balance in the long run assumes simultaneous sustainability of the dynamics of net export incl. balance of labor income and transfers and of the conditions of servicing the existing NFA of a country. This method combines both the traditional macroeconomic interpretation of external balance through macrofactors of the dynamics of current account balance and microeconomic approach of an investor financing the current account deficit of a certain country and/or its negative NFA. Besides, attention is drawn to the fact that under certain circumstances the costs/yields related to NFA may be more significant for the dynamics of NFA and sustainability of external balance than the traditionally observed balance of net export.

In macroeconomic terms, the ratio of net export to GDP (nx_t) is given by the sum of differences between the rate of private savings (s_t) and investments

(i_t) and by the ratio of the balance of government revenues (t_t) and expenditures (g_t) to actual GDP:

$$nx_t = (s_t - i_t) + (t_t - g_t) \tag{3}$$

In general, sustainability of net export assumes that the dynamics of particular factors behind the balance of net export is consistent with the maintenance of internal and external balance and with the maintenance of the financial system stability in the long run. This condition is satisfied if the dynamics of net export is not a source of forced monetary or fiscal restriction, significant depreciation/devaluation of domestic currency or enforced change in the exchange rate policy, jump decrease in consumption and investments and/or significant increase in public debt/forced sale of state property. In an economic model this condition can be specified as a magnitude, or as a ratio of parameters describing the dynamics of particular elements of the economic system in the long run (for advanced economies see e.g. Freund, 2000).

In transition economies two types of fundamentally different development of net export can be identified. In traditional terms, deficit of net export is typical of transition economies – at least in the initial stage – resulting from a high rate of investments in relation to the rate of savings (common influence of undercapitalization of these economies and potential effect of retained savings leading to a fast increase in consumption) or from the deficit of public budgets reflecting the costs of economy transformation in various forms or resulting from a lack of fiscal discipline. The financing of net export deficit by the net inflow of foreign capital logically leads to the worsening of NFA and to the necessity of covering the incurred costs.

However, the experience of many, particularly Asian export-oriented economies shows that this scenario cannot be generalized and that it is to accept a somewhat paradoxical situation when, in spite of the above discussed influences, transition/emerging economies have the long-term surplus of net export as a result of the high rate of savings or restricted role of the government e.g. in the social area at simultaneous frequent interventions of the government in the maintenance of export competitiveness of companies within the exchange rate policy. So they are able to finance current account deficits of some advanced economies while their NFA is improving over time and its service costs are decreasing.

II. Sustainability of NFA in the Short and Long Run and Costs of Financing of Net Foreign Assets

A more detailed specification of the influence of costs/yields of the existing NFA on the relation between NFA and GDP requires to differentiate between the particular types of returns on foreign assets and costs of foreign liabilities. The rearrangement of equation (2) results in this relation:

$$\frac{NFA_T}{GDP_t} = \frac{NX_t}{GDP_t} + \frac{TR_t}{GDP_t} +$$

$$+\frac{[1+ir_t^{FA}(1-L_T^{FA}) + (div_t^{FA} + rp_t^{FA})L_T^{FA} + cg_t^{FA} + er_t^{FA}(1\text{-}K_T^{FA})(1 + ir_t^{FA}(1-L_T^{FA}) + (div_t^{FA} + rp_t^{FA})L_T^{FA} + cg_t^{FA})]FA_{T\text{-}1}}{(1+\gamma_t).GDP_{t\text{-}1}} -$$

$$-\frac{[1+ir_t^{FL}(1-L_T^{FL}) + (div_t^{FL} + rp_t^{FL})L_T^{FL} + cg_t^{FL} + er_t^{FL}(1\text{-}K_T^{FL})(1 + ir_t^{FL}(1-L_T^{FL}) + (div_t^{FL} + rp_t^{FL})L_T^{FL} + cg_t^{FL})]FL_{T\text{-}1}}{(1+\gamma_t).GDP_{t\text{-}1}} =$$

$$= \frac{NX_t}{GDP_t} + \frac{TR_t}{GDP_t} + \frac{1+\beta_t^{FA}}{1+\gamma_t}.\frac{FA_{T\text{-}1}}{GDP_{t\text{-}1}} - \frac{1+\beta_t^{FL}}{1+\gamma_t}.\frac{FL_{T\text{-}1}}{GDP_{t\text{-}1}} \tag{4}$$

where the superscript *FA* and/or *FL* identifies for the variables *ir*, *div*, *rp* and *cg* the rate of interest yield, rate of dividend yield, rate of retained profits and rate of capital profits/losses from foreign assets and/or liabilities, K_T^{FA} and/or K_T^{FL} expressed the ratio of foreign assets and/or liabilities denominated in domestic currency in total foreign assets and/or liabilities, L_T^{FA} and/or L_T^{FL} is the ratio of property foreign assets and/or liabilities in total foreign assets and/or liabilities, and β_t^{FA} and/or β_t^{FL} is the return on foreign assets and/or liabilities expressed by the term $ir_t\left(1-L_T\right) + (div_t + rp_t)L_T + cg_t + er_t(1\text{-}K_T)(1+ir_t\left(1-L_T\right) + (div_t + rp_t)L_T + cg_t)$.

The sustainability of NFA requires a combination of yields and ratios specified in equation (4) that will not cause an increase in the ratio of NFA to GDP to such a level that would be assessed by foreign investors – providing the financing and/or refinancing capital – as the level threatening the full return of their capital according to conditions agreed on with the residents of a country as net foreign debtors. In the economies that have problems with the fast growing negative ratio between NFA and GDP the restoration of the balance can be seen as the process of satisfying the condition of sustainability in two gradual phases. In the short run the sustainability of NFA necessarily requires the stabilization of the ratio between NFA and GDP (i.e. $\Delta \frac{NFA_T}{GDP_t} = 0$). Then it must hold good that:

$$\frac{NX_t}{GDP_t} + \frac{TR_t}{GDP_t} = -\frac{\alpha_t - \gamma_t}{1+\gamma_t} \cdot \frac{NFA_{T-1}}{GDP_{t-1}} \tag{5}$$

and/or

$$\frac{NX_t}{GDP_t} + \frac{TR_t}{GDP_t} = -\frac{\beta_t^{FA} - \gamma_t}{1+\gamma_t} \cdot \frac{FA_{T-1}}{GDP_{t-1}} + \frac{\beta_t^{FL} - \gamma_t}{1+\gamma_t} \cdot \frac{FL_{T-1}}{GDP_{t-1}} \tag{6}$$

The form of sustainability condition in the short run explicitly shows that in order to satisfy this condition, the economy is assumed to be able to generate resources to cover the costs of negative net foreign asset position. The satisfaction of sustainability condition is rather complicated because the parameters defining this condition are given in the short run and the country cannot use any conventional adjustment mechanisms for the restoration of the balance. It is not surprising because of price and wage rigidity that the price- and income-adjustment mechanism cannot be effective enough in the short run while the exchange rate mechanism need not be efficient either because due to J-curve effect and negative NFA the depreciation of domestic currency causes a parallel worsening of net export and an increase in costs paid from NFA. On the other hand, under such situation the importance of the exchange rate adjustment process is as follows: if the investors gradually correctly assess the worsening of external relations and project it in domestic currency depreciation, a fast increase in the negative ratio of NFA to GDP (caused by both the influence of domestic currency depreciation in a situation of the short open foreign exchange position of a country and own costs of NFA) may be accompanied by positive real effects such as increase in the foreign competitiveness of domestic exports and/or decrease in the competitiveness of foreign imports (i.e. by overcoming the J-curve effect).

In general, the instantaneous capacity of an economy to stabilize the ratio of NFA to GDP is given by the percentage costs of NFA on the one hand, and on the other hand by competitiveness of an economy in the world market and/or by the balance between public and private savings and investments expressed as the ratio of net export surplus to GDP and last but not least, by the real performance of an economy as a certain rate of economic growth. Equation (5) clearly illustrates that the sign and the required value of the ratio of net export, labor income and transfers to GDP leading to the stabilization of the ratio of NFA to GDP are dependent on whether the nominal economic growth rate is higher or lower than the total percentage costs paid from NFA (i.e. whether γ_t is higher or smaller than α_t). This condition suggests that the economy can generate resources to cover the costs of NFA either in the absolute sense of the word by means of a sufficient surplus of net export, labor income and transfer balance or by the fast economic growth rate at the simultaneously reasonably low deficit of net export, labor income and transfer balance.

In the short run the capacity of an economy to stabilize the ratio of NFA to GDP is largely influenced to what extent the actual phase of the economic cycle is pulled by domestic or foreign demand. An ideal situation is the relatively fast economic growth rate pulled by export (i.e. by foreign demand) when net export is improved and parallelly the value of the term α_t - γ_t decreases. An essential condition of this situation is that export dynamics overtakes the growth of unit wage costs and consumption initiated by export incomes (i.e. aggregate demand meets with the highly elastic function of aggregate supply). However, the combination of sharp economic deceleration stemming from foreign demand and of the fast import dynamics resulting from high domestic private/public consumer and investment demand (i.e. aggregate demand decreases at the highly inelastic function of aggregate supply) is problematic from the aspect of satisfying the condition of stabilization. Then the satisfaction of sustainability condition in the short run necessarily requires the implementation of restrictive fiscal and monetary policy aimed at a jump decrease in domestic absorption and unit wage costs.

It is to assume in the long run that the satisfaction of the short-term condition of stabilization of the ratio of NFA to GDP is not sufficient to maintain investor's confidence and that the sustainability of NFA necessarily requires a trend decrease in the ratio of NFA to GDP to a safer level (i.e. in the long run $\Delta\frac{\mathrm{NFA_T}}{\mathrm{GDP_t}} > 0$), while the rate of decreasing this ratio is sufficient to maintain foreign investor's confidence. In the horizon of subsequent years it must hold good that:

$$\frac{\mathrm{NX_t}}{\mathrm{GDP_t}} + \frac{\mathrm{TR_t}}{\mathrm{GDP_t}} + \frac{\alpha_t - \gamma_t}{1+\gamma_t} \cdot \frac{\mathrm{NFA_{T\text{-}1}}}{\mathrm{GDP_{t\text{-}1}}} \geq \delta_t \tag{7}$$

and/or

$$\frac{NX_t}{GDP_t} + \frac{TR_t}{GDP_t} + \frac{\beta_t^{FA} - \gamma_t}{1 + \gamma_t} \cdot \frac{FA_{T\text{-}1}}{GDP_{t\text{-}1}} - \frac{\beta_t^{FL} - \gamma_t}{1 + \gamma_t} \cdot \frac{FL_{T\text{-}1}}{GDP_{t\text{-}1}} \geq \delta_t \tag{8}$$

where δ_t expresses the minimum rate of a decrease in the ratio of NFA to GDP (in percentage points) acceptable by foreign investors for further financing of the negative NFA of a country. The satisfaction of the long-term condition of sustainability assumes that simultaneous relations among the particular variables within the sustainability condition are of such an economic character that shows the capacity of overall restoration of the competitive position of an economy in the world market through the adaptation of exchange rate, price and income relations in an economy that will enable the economy to cut the costs of NFA by the accumulation of surpluses of the balance of current account. It will necessarily bring about a decrease in unit costs, restoration of the balance of private savings and investments and fiscal consolidation. On the contrary, the success of this process is threatened by long-term strangulation of economic growth that is connected with a decrease in aggregate demand caused by the restriction of private and public expenditure.

A decrease in the ratio of NFA to GDP must inevitably be "worked off" through the (increasing) surplus of net export, i.e. besides expenditure restriction particularly by the adaptation (restoration of competitiveness) of the supply side of an economy. It is basically possible only when the dynamics of economic growth is pulled by export and if the balance restoration does not exclusively lie in the restriction of domestic absorption. Last but not least, the process of balance restoration is related to the rate of a decrease in the costs of the negative NFA of a country either on the side of net interest costs and paid out dividends or value changes. From this aspect there arises a cardinal question to what extent the costs of NFA are given exogenously and/or to what extent they can be influenced by own adjustment processes. A specific issue is the relationship between status or flow criteria of external balance (NFA of a country and/or the ratio of net export (current account) to GDP) and risk premium paid by domestic economic agents from foreign liabilities. An interesting problem is the character of the relation between net export and profitability ratios of domestic exporters through the effect of the ownership of exporting companies. Last but not least, it is also the overall importance of exchange rate adaptation for the restoration of competitiveness within unit wage costs and for sustainability of the costs of NFA.

III. Analysis of Economic Conditions of Realization of Net Yields/Costs from Negative Net Foreign Assets in Advanced and Transition Economies

A Condition of Reaching the Positive Balance of Yields at Negative NFA in the Context of Sustainability of NFA

The dynamics of balance of yields results from the specific constellation of factors influencing net interest and dividend yields and net reinvested profits from foreign assets and liabilities. It is to expect that under normal circumstances the negative NFA is connected with the payment of net costs within the balance of yields. So the negative NFA of a country may generate the surplus of yield balance only if the following condition is satisfied that the ratio of interest and dividend yields to the rate of reinvested profits from foreign assets and liabilities (including exchange rate profits/losses) is higher than the own relations of foreign liabilities and assets:

$$\frac{ir_t^{FA}(1-L_T^{FA})+(div_t^{FA}+rp_t^{FA})L_T^{FA}+er_t^{FA}(1\text{-}K_T^{FA})(1+ir_t^{FA}(1-L_T^{FA})+(div_t^{FA}+rp_t^{FA})L_T^{FA})}{ir_t^{FL}(1-L_T^{FL})+(div_t^{FL}+rp_t^{FL})L_T^{FL}+er_t^{FL}(1\text{-}K_T^{FL})(1+ir_t^{FL}(1-L_T^{FL})+(div_t^{FL}+rp_t^{FL})L_T^{FL})} > \frac{FL_{T-1}}{FA_{T-1}} \quad (9)$$

It is questionable to what extent this condition can be fulfilled in general or whether from the economic aspect there exist differences in a possibility of fulfilling this condition between advanced and transition economies. Some significant differences in some parameters of the economic system seem to exist between advanced and transition economies, causing that this condition is fulfilled rather scarcely, even in advanced economies; on the contrary, transition economies should take into account that their costs paid from negative NFA may be higher in relation to GDP than it would result from the ratio of negative NFA to GDP.

Differences in Property and/or Debt Structure of Foreign Assets and Liabilities

Negative NFA is naturally connected with the negative balance of yields within the balance of payments. As demonstrated on an example of the U.S.

economy by Tille (2003) and Higgins, Klitgaard and Tille (2005), under some circumstances the economy may show in the long run the surplus of yield balance (excluding the other items within the balance of yields that are not connected with net costs of NFA) in spite of the significantly negative NFA. This paradox stems first of all from a specific constellation of the structure of foreign assets and liabilities as the ratio between assets and/or liabilities of property type (L_T^{FA} and/or L_T^{FL}) and debt type [$(1 - L_T^{FA})$, and/or $(1 - L_T^{FL})$], in the total foreign assets and/or liabilities. The authors reported the relatively high share of property investments (particularly of foreign direct investments) on the side of foreign assets and on the other hand, the relatively high share of foreign liabilities of debt type (i.e. $L_T^{FA} > L_T^{FL}$). The significant share of foreign direct investments on the assets side is a result of the historical position of the USA as a net exporter of capital in the form of net foreign direct investments. It can be considered as a typical feature of advanced economies with the long-term current account surplus. On the other hand – contrary to the practice of advanced economies – the negative NFA of the USA and a high share of debt foreign liabilities are a result of accumulations of current account deficit and specific mode of its financing through the inflow of mostly debt capital leading to an increasing share of public and private debt in the hands of foreign investors.

The effect of the structure of foreign assets and/or liabilities is a significant factor potentially differentiating the dynamics of net interest and dividend yields of foreign assets and liabilities incl. yields in the form of retained profits from the own dynamics of NFA resulting from the accumulation of current account deficits. It is to note that the relatively high share of property foreign assets may generate the significantly higher average return on foreign assets compared to the average return on foreign liabilities where less costly debt foreign liabilities are dominant (i.e. it holds good that $ir_t^{FA}(1 - L_t^{FA}) + (div_t^{FA} + rp_t^{FA})L_t^{FA} > ir_t^{FL}(1 - L_t^{FL}) + (div_t^{FL} + rp_t^{FL})L_t^{FL}$). This effect can traditionally be connected with demands on generally higher return on own capital compared to the costs of debt capital (i.e. it generally holds good $div + rp > ir$). Especially in foreign direct investments the capital is traditionally directed from advanced economies to developing countries while higher marginal efficiency of capital (real return on capital employed) is expected in less developed markets (consequently it holds good for advanced countries that $div_t^{FA} + rp_t^{FA} > div_t^{FL} + rp_t^{FL}$). Important is also the time profile of realized foreign direct investments when higher return on property assets can be realized in transition economies only after some time elapsing from the investment realization (at the time of investment maturity). Last but not least, the effect of transition economy is also reflected in the price of mergers and acquisitions in these markets, which is usually underestimated in relation to prices paid in advanced markets due to the investor's demands on a higher risk premium, average worse financial performance of acquired companies and due to the frequent controlled undervaluation of the currency of a host country in relation to the investor's currency in a certain phase of economic transformation. The final impact on the interest and dividend yield of foreign assets/liabilities is related to the method of repricing of foreign assets/liabilities to the real value including the calculation of exchange rate profits/losses. It holds good that full repricing to the real value completely eliminates the significance of this effect; on the other hand, continuous repricing of investments, in which the liquid secondary market does not exist, to the real value is not quite common in practice.

Considering the factors influencing costs of NFA in transition economies it is typical that they are in the position of significant net recipients of foreign capital through foreign direct investments that, on the side of liabilities of NFA, usually dominate above foreign resources of debt character. A common feature of transition economies is also a significant ratio of foreign exchange reserves on the side of foreign assets that results from the activity of central banks when influencing the exchange rate through exchange rate interventions (see Brůna and Durčáková, 2012). Such policy is based on an assumption that a sustainable source of economic growth in small transition economies is mostly the dynamics of growth of net export, not a consumption. Therefore it is symptomatic that central banks intervene in the foreign exchange market in order to maintain competitiveness not only in the system of fixed exchange rates that is applied in the first phase of transformation but also in systems of floating exchange rate (either directly in the wholesale foreign exchange market or through special operations outside the public market).

It is to assume that with regard to the structure of foreign assets and liabilities transition economies have to pay relatively high costs from negative NFA. Their current account deficit may become hardly sustainable also when the dynamics of net export does not show any features of non-sustainability or the current account deficit may show long-term significant deficits in spite of the economy transition to an economic phase characterized by net export surplus. Sustainability of the negative NFA of these countries is influenced by the fact to what extent the costs of foreign liabilities in the form of foreign direct investments are composed of paid-out dividends and to what extent they are calculated on the basis of reinvested profit that does not produce an instantaneous pressure on domestic currency depreciation. It is possible to imagine a situation paradoxical at a glance when the worsening NFA and net export are accompanied by appreciation of domestic currency reacting primarily to improving but still negative net export.

Problem of Interest Rate Differential Endogeneity in Relation to Currency Structure of Foreign Assets and Liabilities and Risk Premium

Another factor of costs of NFA is the spread of interest yields between foreign assets and liabilities of debt character, the level and dynamics of which over time are given by the currency structure of these assets and liabilities and collected/paid risk premium. The factor of currency structure determines to what extent the interest yield of debt foreign assets and liabilities is exogenously given by the position and slope of yield curves of risk-free interest rates in foreign markets and/or yield curves of foreign currencies constituting the portfolio of debt foreign assets and liabilities, and to what extent net interest costs are influenced by domestic factors and/or dynamics of domestic yield curve of risk-free interest rates. In case that foreign assets and liabilities are denominated exclusively in foreign currency (i.e. $K_T^{FA} = K_T^{FL} = 0$), the risk-free interest yield of foreign assets and liabilities is fully exogenous and domestic factors do not have any influence on net costs paid from debt assets and liabilities (except potential differences in risk premiums of home debtors). A necessary condition is that due to its size or international importance the economy does not have the potential to influence, through the dynamics of domestic macrofactors, the dynamics of economic fundaments and behaviour of central banks in foreign countries and so to influence changes in the position and slope of yield curves in international money and bond markets.

However, in large and relatively closed advanced economies whose currency is in the position of reserve and/or invoice or investment currency there exists a significant disproportion between the currency structure of foreign assets and liabilities when the ratio of domestic currency in foreign liabilities may be significantly higher than in foreign assets (i.e. K_T^{FA} and $K_T^{FL} > 0$, when K_T^{FA} is significantly smaller that K_T^{FL}). In this case the risk-free interest yield of foreign liabilities is endogenous in such a sense that it is determined for the most part by domestic factors (dynamics of inflation and economic growth) and by a reaction of monetary policy to these factors (i.e. setting the main policy rate) that jointly influence changes in the position and slope of domestic yield curve over time. This is applicable to foreign assets to a limited extent only. The dynamics of net interest costs is determined for the most part by the rate of correlation of yield curves in the domestic and foreign market (and/or of the hypothetical yield curve corresponding to the structure of foreign assets from the aspect of currencies, maturity and undertaken risk) or by the rate of correlation of the factors behind the dynamics of yield curves (hence it is a problem of synchronization of the economic and inflation cycle and trend changes in main policy rates).

In general it is to assume that in reserve currencies the interest yield of foreign liabilities is relatively low in comparison with the interest yield of foreign assets (i.e. $ir_t^{FA} > ir_t^{FL}$) because in international financial markets advanced countries generally pay low (also negative) real interest rates in the context of relatively weak economic growth (long-term stagnation in some cases) and/or low marginal efficiency of investments, they benefit from a low inflation premium with regard to the low and stable rate of inflation, and last but not least, they pay low risk premiums thanks to usually high credit rating and relatively high risk aversion of investors to emerging markets (currencies). If at the same time the foreign assets are composed of a significant part of assets from emerging economies that work with generally higher real interest rate, expected inflation and risk premium, advanced economies may collect positive interest yields although their net position resulting from debt foreign assets and liabilities is negative. Such a situation may be particularly relevant for advanced countries with the high public debt that is financed for the most part by the inflow of foreign capital that is denominated in domestic currency at the same time (the example of the USA).

Last but not least, NFA and balance of yields of advanced countries are influenced by a successful process of convergence of transition economies that is connected with the nominal appreciation of currencies of transition countries. It may be caused by the fact that in spite of potential negative NFA, their foreign exchange position may in fact be “long” as a consequence of the high ratio of foreign liabilities denominated in domestic currency, i.e. from the aspect of future exchange rate development these economies are in the position of a speculator on domestic currency depreciation. Depreciation of their currencies in the context convergence of transition economies to advanced ones logically leads to exchange rate profits improving their NFA and net interest yields. In small open economies (a typical feature of the majority of transition economies) it is considered as logical that the interest yields of foreign assets and liabilities (and their spread) are given exogenously by virtue of their currency structure because their currency is not in the position of reserve, invoice or investment currency in foreign markets. Hence it is not to expect that their debt foreign liabilities are denominated in domestic currency to a larger extent and that their economy is in the "long" speculative position within NFA. From the aspect of speculation on future trend of domestic currency these economies are in the situation of a speculator on domestic currency appreciation with regard to the negative NFA given by the current account cumulated deficit. The NFA of transition economies may however be influenced significantly by a long-term positive differential between domestic and foreign interest rate that makes domestic economic agents prefer foreign currencies at the denomination of bank credits/bond issues at the cost of credits/issues in domestic currency. Economic agents liberate themselves from the restrictive aspect of high domestic nominal interest rates (even though the real level of interest rates may be low) by cutting the interest costs of financing at a simultaneous increase in exposure to exchange rate risk while they get to the same position as a speculator within the carry trades strategy. Regardless whether these credits are granted mostly by domestic or foreign banks (the point is who is affected by credit risk resulting from the fact that in the case of domestic currency depreciation the rate of default from the credit portfolio denominated in foreign currency increases) the dynamics of NFA caused by the massive inflow of foreign debt capital is related to the rate of worsening net export by the inflow of foreign capital as a result of high import intensity of the economy and/or of the low export performance of assets financed by the inflow of foreign capital. Obviously, in this connection the inflow of foreign capital will cause a pressure on an increase in the ratio of the costs of more costly debt liabilities with longer maturity in total foreign assets. On the other hand, it is not quite evident to what extent an increase in foreign liabilities will cause an increase in foreign assets. In this sense two basic scenarios can be identified: in case that the trend of imports is relatively low and the export performance of assets is high (a typical case of financing corporate investments in a new production capacity), due to the inflow of capital it is to assume a pressure on domestic currency appreciation that will subsequently cause a pressure on the socialization of losses of domestic holders of assets in foreign currency or exporters through exchange rate interventions of central bank. In such a case there does not occur a significant worsening of NFA because foreign assets of central bank increase rapidly at a simultaneous decrease in foreign assets of private holders. As a result of domestic currency appreciation the country takes exchange rate profits, not only on the level of negative NFA but also within net costs paid from it. On the other hand, there arises a negative differential between interest yields of foreign assets and liabilities because foreign assets are invested in assets with a lower risk premium (the ratio of low-risk foreign exchange reserves in foreign assets increases) than is the risk premium of granted foreign-currency bank credits. In case that the trend of imports is high and the export performance of assets is low (a typical case of financing consumption), there are neither appreciation tendencies due to the worsening of net export nor a change in the structure of foreign assets in favour of central bank assets. Therefore the NFA is worsening rapidly, which may cause depreciation pressures on domestic currency after some time with subsequent exchange rate losses at the level of NFA and net costs paid from negative foreign asset position. On the contrary, the preference of foreign-currency resources of financing domestic private or government consumption and investments indicates the problem of endogeneity of the interest yield of foreign liabilities that in transition economies results from the endogenous nature of risk premium which is potentially a strongly nonlinear function of the ratio of negative NFA to GDP. The negative differential between interest yields of foreign assets and liabilities need not be only a matter of the differential of economic fundaments between transition and advanced economies, it may reflect confidence in the sustainability of NFA on the part of foreign investors providing financial funds and reflecting the increased probability of country's default.

IV. Analysis of the Costs and Sustainability of Net Foreign Asset Position of the Czech Republic in 2000-2011

The empirical part of the study contains the analysis of dynamics of NFA of the Czech Republic (CR) and analysis of factors that influence the dynamics of costs paid from NFA of CR in the period 2000-2011. Figure 1 clearly illustrates the trend worsening of NFA to GDP ratio from values around -5% to more than -50%. Subsequently, Figure 2 shows that from the economic aspect the cause behind this trend is that domestic economy is not able to generate resources as the surplus of net export, balance of current and capital transfers and balance of labor that will enable to continuously cover the costs of negative NFA as the negative balance of dividends, interests and reinvested profit. A disproportion between economic resources and costs of NFA reached about -5 to -6% of GDP by 2004, since then, in connection with a sharp improvement in net export, it has changed to the level of -2 to -3%. Figure 1 documents that this disproportion requires the acquisition of additional financial resources from foreign investors, distinctly above the growth rate of nominal GDP because the relation between foreign liabilities and GDP continually increases while the foreign assets to GDP ratio stagnates.

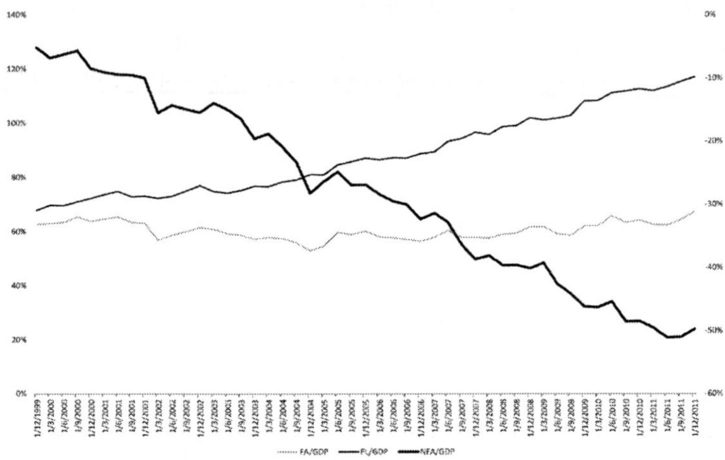

Source: CNB, my own calculations.

Figure 1. Net foreign asset position (right axis), foreign assets and foreign liabilities in relation to GDP (in %, quarterly data).

This situation is not caused by the generally low export performance of domestic economy (the surplus of net export has gradually increased to ca. 4% of GDP), on the contrary, it is caused by the relatively high costs domestic economy has to pay from rapidly increasing negative NFA. Figure 2 shows the trend of an increase in the costs of negative NFA while they culminated at the end of the studied period when they reached the level of 8% GDP. Because in the framework of available data no data are available on realized capital profits/losses a modified version of β_t^* defined in the theoretical part of the study is used for the analysis of the causes of high costs paid from NFA:

$$\frac{\text{costs of NFA}}{GDP_t} = \frac{\beta_t^{*FA} FA_t - \beta_t^{*FL} FL_t}{GDP_t} \tag{10}$$

where $\beta_t^{*FA} = ir_t^{FA}(1 - L_T^{FA}) + (div_t^{FA} + rp_t^{FA})L_T^{FA} + er_t^{FA}(1+ir_t^{FA}(1 - L_T^{FA}) + (div_t^{FA} + rp_t^{FA})L_T^{FA})$ and $\beta_t^{*FL} = ir_t^{FL}(1 - L_T^{FL}) + (div_t^{FL} + rp_t^{FL})L_T^{FL} + er_t^{FL}(1+ir_t^{FL}(1 - L_T^{FL}) + (div_t^{FL} + rp_t^{FL})L_T^{FL})$.

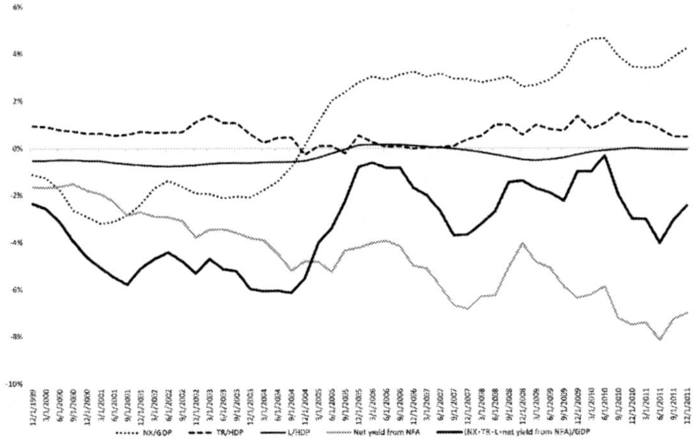

Source: CNB, my own calculations.

Figure 2. Net export, balance of transfers, returns on labor and NFA yield in relation to GDP (in %, quarterly data).

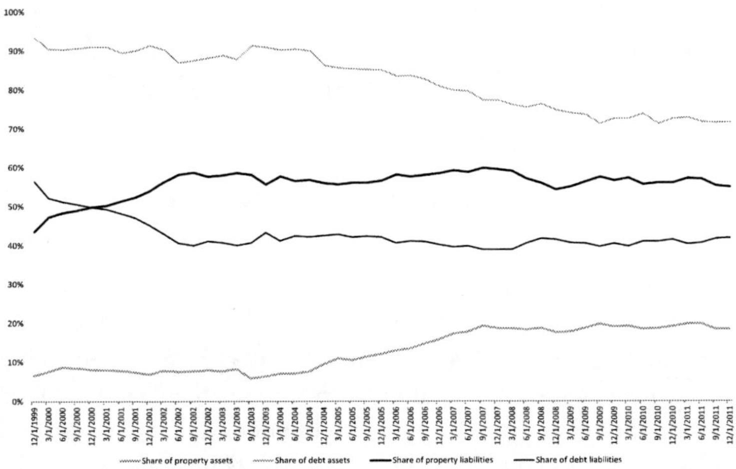

Source: CNB, my own calculations.

Figure 3. Structure of foreign assets and liabilities (in %, quarterly data).

Obviously, the CR shows typical features of transition economies, i.e. the costs paid from foreign liabilities are relatively high compared to returns on foreign assets ($\beta_t^{*FA} < \beta_t^{*FL}$). One of the causes is (see Figure 3) that the economically costly capital of property type accounts for ca. 55-60% of foreign liabilities, which is given by the long-term positive balance of foreign direct investment inflow and subsequent reinvestment of returns on these assets while this capital accounts max. for 20% of foreign assets, which logically stems from the still relatively low activity of domestic investors in foreign markets in the framework of foreign investments (i.e. $L_T^{FA} < L_T^{FL}$). On the other hand, as for foreign assets, potentially less profitable debt assets are clearly dominant consisting of Czech National Bank's foreign exchange reserves (the share of 35-50% in foreign debt assets).

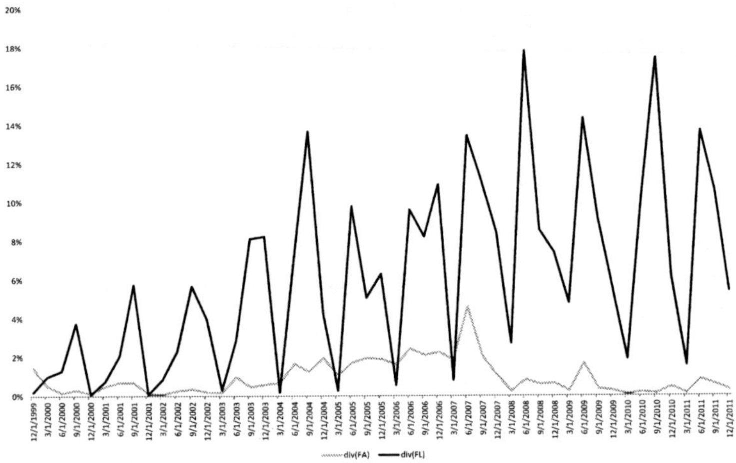

Source: CNB, my own calculations.

Figure 4. Dividend yields from foreign assets and liabilities (in %, quarterly data, annualized).

Besides the unfavourable structure of foreign assets and liabilities a high spread between dividend yields of property foreign liabilities and assets is behind the high costs of NFA (i.e. $(div_t^{FL} - div_t^{FA}) > 0$ (see Figure 4). On average, a differential of dividend yields is ca. 5 percentage points. In spite of the high volatility of dividend yields of liabilities the average spread had been maintained on an acceptable level of ca. 3-4 percentage points until 2007 while with the onset of financial crisis this spread significantly increased to the level of around 7-8 percentage points due to the steep slump of dividend yield of foreign assets when the returns on foreign liabilities stagnated and/or decreased only moderately. The financial and subsequent economic crisis seems not to substantially affect the profitability ratios of domestic firms owned by foreign proprietors, which allows them to pursue the policy of stable dividend yields while the profitability ratios of domestic acquisitions in other countries were substantially weakened with a natural impact on dividend yields of foreign assets.

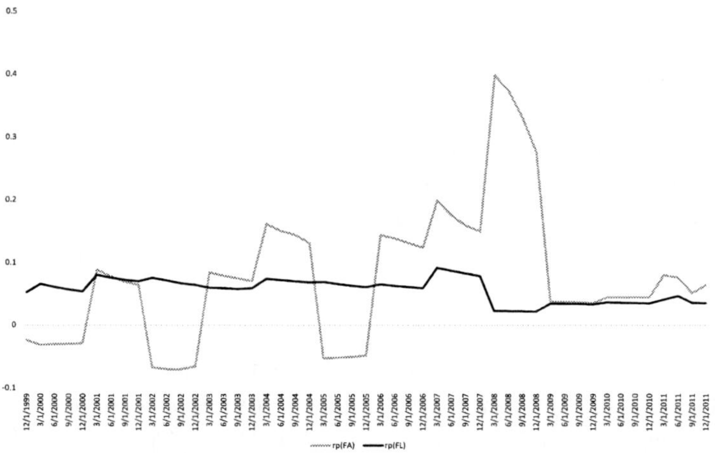

Source: CNB, my own calculations.

Figure 5. The rate of reinvested profit from foreign assets and liabilities (in %, quarterly data, annualized).

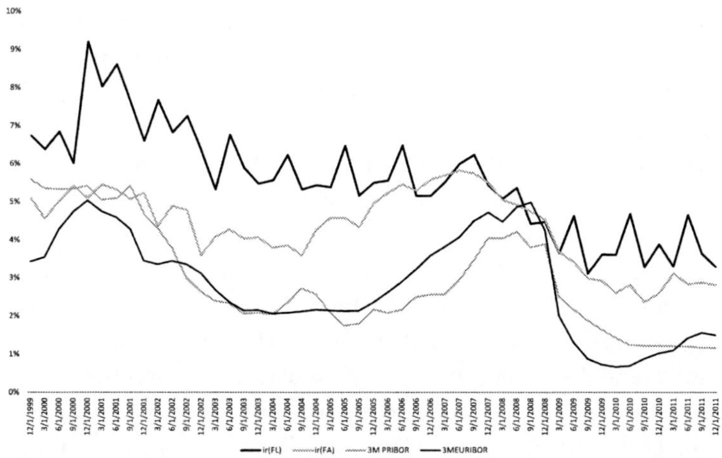

Source: CNB, my own calculations.

Figure 6. Interest yield of foreign assets and liabilities and main reference money market interest rates (in %, quarterly data, annualized).

However, this assumption appears to be correct only in the case of a decrease in the profitability ratios of nationals' foreign investments when Figure 5 confirms, besides a decrease in dividend yield, also a significant decrease in the rate of reinvested profit from foreign assets compared to the years 2006-08. It is also obvious from the rate of reinvested profit from foreign liabilities when the pre-crisis level of the rate of reinvested profit around 7% sharply decreases to the values comparable with the rate of reinvested profit from foreign assets, i.e. to ca. 3-4%. It means that it is possible to sustain the stable dividend yield of foreign liabilities only at the expense of a decrease in the rate of reinvested profit. From the aspect of the costs paid from negative NFA the effect of the rate of reinvested profit is positive because the average rate of reinvested profit from foreign assets is higher than that from foreign liabilities (i.e. $rp_t^{FA} > rp_t^{FL}$) by two percentage points. As stated above, the effect of this fact on a decrease in the costs is significantly restricted by a low share of assets of property type in the total volume of foreign assets.

Last but not least, a positive differential between interest yields of foreign debt liabilities and assets is behind the high costs paid from NFA (Figure 6). The differential between interest yields was high especially at the beginning of the studied period until 2005, when the high share of CNB's foreign exchange reserves in foreign assets culminated and when interest rates in foreign markets decreased. A subsequent decrease in the average differential of interest yields was influenced by an increase in foreign interest rates and by the improving domestic economy, which limits the credit premium paid by domestic firms, and also by a gradual increase in the CR´s rating that is reflected in a decrease in the credit premium of bonds issued by the government in foreign markets. Nevertheless, the differential between interest yields of foreign assets and liabilities reached the level around -1.3 percentage points in the studied period.

From the aspect of NFA sustainability, it is to state ultimately that under current circumstances the CR is not able to ensure permanently either short-term or long-term condition of sustainability. The basic problem is the existing positive differential between total returns on foreign liabilities and assets, the components of which were analyzed above, and the growth rate of GDP that does not reach the returns on foreign liabilities in most cases (Figure 7). After the inclusion of domestic economy's capacity to generate resources to cover these costs it is evident (Figure 8) that determinants on the side of net costs paid from NFA (see the right side of equation 6) usually exceed the resources produced by the CR economy (the left side of equation 6). The majority of the points in Fig. 8 lie above the straight line drawn at an angle of 45°, indicating that the short-term condition of NFA sustainability is reached. Ultimately, it is to expect the gradual worsening of NFA to GDP ratio, and/or the stabilization of this ratio necessarily assumes a significant improvement in the ratio of surplus output balance to GDP and GDP growth rate at a simultaneous decrease in the negative differential of yields of foreign assets and liabilities.

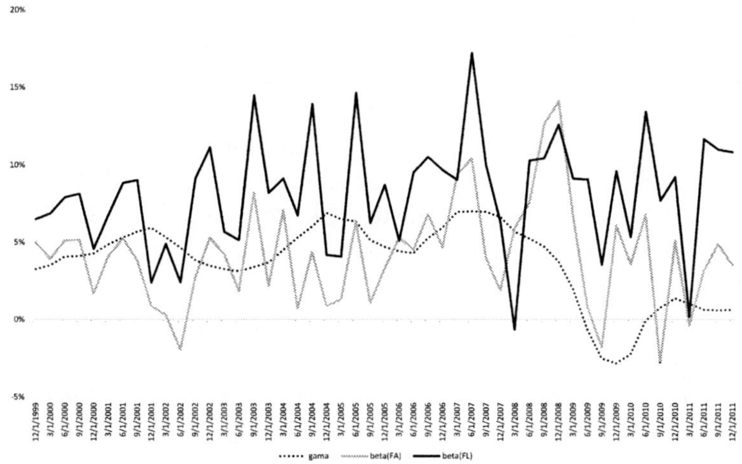

Source: CNB, my own calculations.

Figure 7. The values of $\boldsymbol{\beta_t^{*FA}}, \boldsymbol{\beta_t^{*FL}}$ **and** $\boldsymbol{\gamma_t}$ (in %, quarterly data, annualized).

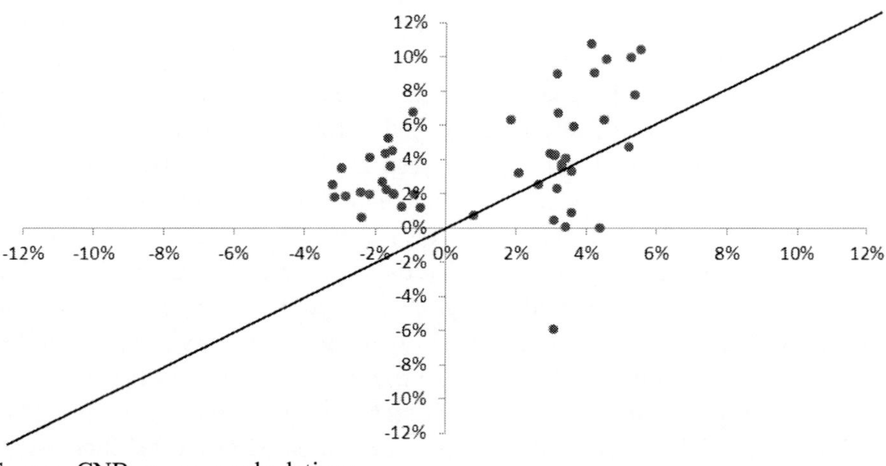

Source: CNB, my own calculations.

Figure 8. The relation $(NX_t+TR_t+L_t)/GDP_t$ (x-axis) against $-\frac{\beta_t^{FA}-\gamma_t}{1+\gamma_t}.\frac{FA_{T-1}}{GDP_{t-1}}+\frac{\beta_t^{FL}-\gamma_t}{1+\gamma_t}.\frac{FL_{T-1}}{GDP_{t-1}}$ (y-axis) (in %, quarterly data).

The magnitude of correlation coefficients between the particular factors of the NFA sustainability condition incl. the dynamics of CZK and EUR reference interest rates (Table 1) indicates some relationships that are crucial for the long-term sustainability of NFA in the CR. According to the logic of the correlation coefficient calculation these relationships need not necessarily represent the existence of a causal correlation between the particular variables but only the common (trend) direction of movement. From the aspect of the economy capacity to generate resources reducing the NFA/GDP ratio, firstly it is important that economic growth and the ratio of NX/GDP and/or (NX+TR+L)/GDP are weakly negatively correlated (corr. coeff. -0.38 and -0.45, respectively). The NFA/GDP ratio seems to be anti-cyclic to some extent in relation to the economic cycle evoked by foreign demand, i.e. to the cyclic behavior of net export.

Secondly, as crucial appears the relation between the ratio of NX/GDP and/or (NX+TR+L)/GDP and costs paid by the countries from the increasing volume of foreign liabilities. Due to a significant increase in the ratio of NX/GDP and/or (NX+TR+L)/GDP, and also with regard to a decrease in CZK and EUR reference rates, the concern about the absolute growth of interest rate costs was not proved [respective corr. coeff. -0.78 and -0.79 between NX/GDP and/or (NX+TR+L)/GDP and ir^{FL} and respective corr. coeff. 0.6 and 0.7 for ir^{FL} and IR_{CZK} and/or IR_{EUR}]. The evaluation of a similar correlation with the premium above 3M reference interest rate is complicated because this premium varies not only due to changes in risk premium but also due to changes in the slope of yield curve and term structure of debt foreign liabilities. On the other hand, the increase in the ratio of NX/GDP and/or (NX+TR+L)/GDP is not related with an increase in the rate of reinvested profits (corr. coeff. -0.51 and 0.56, resp.), which indicates at the above discussed decrease in the profitability ratios of property foreign liabilities that the profitability ratios of domestic firms owned by foreign investors are apparently determined to a greater extent by domestic than by foreign demand (corr. coeff. between rp^{FL} and γ is 0.66). From the aspect of (re)financing NFA it is interesting that in spite of the decreasing rate of reinvested and total profits it is possible to identify a positive correlation between the (increasing) ratio of NX/GDP and/or (NX+TR+L)/GDP and the (increasing) rate of dividend yield from foreign liabilities (both corr. coeff. 0.49).

A high positive correlation between the economy's capacity to generate economic resources and the increasing foreign liabilities to GDP ratio can be evaluated explicitly positively [corr. coeff. between NX/GDP and/or (NX+TR+L)/GDP and FL/GDP is 0.89 and 0.91, resp.]. Besides the export performance, the dynamics of dividend costs paid from foreign liabilities is closely correlated with the FL/GDP ratio (corr. coeff. between FL/GDP and div^{FL} is at the level of 0.51).

Table 1. Coefficients of correlation between the factors determining the condition of net foreign asset position sustainability

	er_t	γ_t	IR_{CZK}	IR_{EUR}	div_t^{FA}	div_t^{FL}	rp_t^{FA}	rp_t^{FL}	ir_t^{FA}	ir_t^{FL}	$\frac{NX_t}{GDP_t}$	$\frac{NX_t + TR_t + L_t}{GDP_t}$	$\frac{FA_T}{GDP_t}$	$\frac{FL_T}{GDP_t}$
er_t	1													
γ	-0.22	1												
IR_{CZK}	-0.17	0.47	1											
IR_{EUR}	-0.14	**0.69**	**0.85**	1										
div_t^{FA}	-0.04	0.46	-0.12	0.12	1									
div_t^{FL}	-0.02	-0.13	-0.35	-0.18	0.34	1								
rp_t^{FA}	-0.04	0.24	0.03	0.31	0.21	0.30	1							
rp_t^{FL}	-0.20	**0.66**	0.27	0.33	0.42	-0.30	-0.27	1						
ir_t^{FA}	-0.22	**0.80**	**0.67**	**0.85**	0.45	-0.23	0.20	0.57	1					
ir_t^{FL}	-0.18	**0.60**	**0.70**	**0.65**	0.09	-0.38	-0.22	**0.65**	**0.67**	1				
$\frac{NX_t}{GDP_t}$	0.11	-0.38	**-0.61**	-0.42	0.26	**0.49**	0.31	**-0.51**	-0.33	**-0.78**	1			
$\frac{NX_t + TR_t + L_t}{GDP_t}$	0.12	-0.45	**-0.61**	-0.44	0.19	**0.49**	0.29	**-0.56**	-0.38	**-0.79**	**0.99**	1		
$\frac{FA_T}{GDP_t}$	0.40	-0.46	0.16	-0.02	-0.44	-0.11	-0.27	-0.29	-0.26	-0.01	-0.04	0.04	1	
$\frac{FL_T}{GDP_t}$	0.16	**-0.59**	**-0.64**	-0.51	-0.04	**0.51**	0.29	**-0.66**	**-0.60**	**-0.83**	**0.89**	**0.91**	0.22	1

IR_{CZK} = 3M PRIBOR, IR_{EUR} = 3M EURIBOR.

Source: my own calculations.

As interest rate costs and reinvested profit from foreign liabilities decrease in spite of an increase in the FL/GDP ratio (corr. coeff. between FL/GDP and ir^{FL} and/or rp^{FL} is -0.83 and -0.66, resp.), the increase in the FL/GDP ratio can be connected with the inflow of foreign capital that finances an increasing rate of the dividend yield of foreign liabilities, the level of which exceeds the rate at which the economy is able to generate resources through the positive net export, balance of transfers and net returns on labor.

From the aspect of the dynamics of net costs incurred from NFA, the strong positive correlation between the interest yields of foreign assets and liabilities (corr. coeff. is 0.67) is significant at low levels of the correlation between the rates of reinvested profits and/or dividend yields of foreign assets and liabilities (corr. coeff. between rp^{FA} and rp^{FL} is -0.27 and between div^{FA} and div^{FL} 0.34). At least in the case of interest rate payments, it creates a space for an automatic decrease in the interest rate costs of foreign liabilities at a decreasing interest yield of foreign assets. The interest yield of foreign assets is strongly positively correlated with the level of the EUR reference rate (corr. coeff. 0.85) while the interest yield of foreign liabilities shows a higher correlation with the CZK reference rate (corr. coeff. 0.70). Obviously, whereas the interest yield of foreign assets is exogenous from the aspect of the CR, the interest rate costs paid from foreign liabilities are at least partly of endogenous nature. It is however limited by the fact that the interest rate policy of the CNB basically follows the ECB policy, and so the CZK yield curve is not fully independent of the EUR yield curve. On the other hand, the particular types of yields of foreign assets and/or liabilities mostly have correlation coefficients close to zero, which, from the logic of portfolio diversification, exerts positive effects on the stabilization of changes in the total percent yields and costs of foreign assets and liabilities.

As the relationship of variables based on causal dependence cannot be differentiated by means of correlation coefficients from the relationship with a common trend but without mutual dependence, the econometric analysis was preceded by the analysis of data stationarity (Tab. 2). Using ADF and DF tests, the presence of the unit root was analyzed in time series of variables underlying the condition of NFA sustainability. The series of economic growth, CZK and EUR reference interest rates, rates of reinvested profit from foreign liabilities, interest yield of foreign assets, ratio of NX/GDP and/or (NX+TR+L)/GDP and ratio of FA/GDP and/or FL/GDP seem to be non-stationary at the levels of statistical significance specified below. In all cases their first differences are stationary at high levels of statistical significance.

Table 2. ADF and DF test of the unit root

Variable	Coef.	t-stat.	Model	Lag	Variable	Coef.	t-stat.	Model	Lag
$\mathbf{er_t}$	-0,939*	-6,152	(const, trend)	0	$\mathbf{ir_t^{FA}}$	-0,105	-1,543	(const, trend)	0
γ_t	-0,082	-1,535	(const, trend)	0	$\Delta\mathbf{ir_t^{FA}}$	-1,144***	-7,852	(const, trend)	0
$\Delta\gamma_t$	-0,535**	-3,089	(const, trend)	5	$\mathbf{ir_t^{FL}}$	-0,033	-0,339	(const)	3
$\mathbf{IR_t^{CZK}}$	-0,122	-2,368	(const, trend)	2	$\Delta\ \mathbf{ir_t^{FL}}$	-2,183	-5,891	(const, trend)	2
$\Delta\mathbf{IR_t^{CZK}}$	-0,675*	-4,738	(const, trend)	0	$\frac{\mathbf{NX}_t}{\mathbf{GDP}_t}$	-0,102	-1,7876	(const, trend)	0
$\mathbf{IR_t^{EUR}}$	-0,127	-2,687	(const, trend)	1	$\Delta\frac{\mathbf{NX_t}}{\mathbf{GDP_t}}$	-0,333**	-2,999	(const)	0
$\Delta\mathbf{IR_t^{EUR}}$	-0,442**	-3,537	(const, trend)	0	$\frac{\mathbf{NX_t + TR_t + L_t}}{\mathbf{GDP_t}}$	-0,176	-1,980	(const, trend)	4
$\mathbf{div_t^{FA}}$	-0,369**	-3,217	(const)	0	$\Delta\frac{\mathbf{NX_t + TR_t + L_t}}{\mathbf{GDP_t}}$	-0,845*	-4,442	(const, trend)	3
$\mathbf{div_t^{FL}}$	-0,318*	-2,955	random walk	0	$\frac{\mathbf{FA_T}}{\mathbf{GDP_t}}$	-0,165	-1,752	(const, trend)	0
$\mathbf{rp_t^{FA}}$	-0,151**	-1,947	random walk	0	$\Delta\frac{\mathbf{FA_T}}{\mathbf{GDP_t}}$	-2,188*	-5,766	(const, trend)	3
$\mathbf{rp_t^{FL}}$	-0,306	-3,002	(const, trend)	0	$\frac{\mathbf{FL_T}}{\mathbf{GDP_t}}$	-0.131	-1,832	(const, trend)	5
$\Delta\mathbf{rp_t^{FL}}$	-1,03***	-6,922	(const, trend)	0	$\Delta\frac{\mathbf{FL_T}}{\mathbf{GDP_t}}$	-1,962*	-4,691	(const, trend)	4

*, **, *** - significant at 1%, 5% a 10% level according MacKinnon (1996).
Source: my own calculations.

Taking into account the number of variables in the condition of NFA sustainability, the estimation of econometric model is aimed at the variables that describe the dynamics of economic resources and costs of NFA of the Czech economy. The relationship of the particular variables is analyzed by means of the estimation of parameters of the following econometric model:

$$Y_{j,t} = C_j + \sum_{y=1}^{\infty} \propto_{j,y} Y_{j,t-y} + \sum_{i=1}^{I} \sum_{x=0}^{\infty} \beta_{j,i,t-x} B_{j,i,t-x} + u_{j,t}$$

where Y_t is the j-th explained variable from the set of variables $Y = \{\Delta\frac{NX_t}{GDP_t}, \Delta ir_t^{FL}, \Delta\gamma_t, \Delta rp_t^{FL}, div_t^{FL}, er_t, \Delta\frac{FL_T}{GDP_t}\}$, C is the level constant, $\sum_{y=1}^{\infty} \propto_{j,y} Y_{j,t-y}$ expresses the autoregressive process AR(y), $B_{j,i,t-x}$ is the i-th explaining variable from the set Y, where i≠j, $\beta_{j,i,t-x}$ expresses the estimated parameters of the i-th explaining variable in the j-th explained variable and $u_{j,t}$ is the random component.

The results of the estimation (see Tab. 3) document that stationarized data show a different type of relations in contrast to the above-discussed correlation coefficients. Statistically significant parameters confirm the dynamic adaptation of the particular variables with a time lag of 1-2 years, which corresponds to the horizon of the effective transmission of monetary policy. Equation 1 confirms the above-discussed counteractive movement between the change in NX/GDP and the change in economic growth rate with a lag of seven quarters of the year. The positive relation (with a lag of six quarters of the year) with a change in EUR reference interest rate indirectly indicates the dependence of Czech export dynamics on the foreign economic growth rate when ECB's main refinancing rate and also EUR reference rate follow the cyclic variation of the product. The opposite sign of both parameters suggests that changes in the domestic economic cycle are not synchronous with changes in the cycle of the Eurozone. The changes in economic growth (equation 2) demonstrate a relatively strong relationship to changes in CZK reference rate (with a lag of five quarters of the year) which, unlike the EUR reference rate, counteracts the cycle. Here the connection with the inflation targeting of CNB, or with CNB's reaction function, is evident that assumes the adaptation of repo rate to changes in output gap. The statistically significant influence of changes in exchange rate is very small in quantitative terms, moreover, it has an opposite sign to the expected one.

The impact of changes in NX/GDP ratio and economic growth on the costs incurred from foreign liabilities seems to be very interesting. From the aspect of interest rate costs (equation 3) the effect of an increase in NX/GDP is positive with a lag of one period only, which suggests that financing costs are influenced to a greater extent by the actual cycle in other countries (Eurozone) and by the related cycle of the EUR reference rate than by a decrease in risk premium connected with the Czech economy capacity to generate through growth resources to cover foreign obligations. On the other hand, changes in CZK, not in EUR, reference rate appear statistically significant (lag of two quarters of the year), which confirms the hypothesis of endogeneity of interest rate costs of foreign liabilities. The negative influence of a change in the economic growth rate with a lag of two years is difficult to explain. With a lag of five quarters a significant parameter was also found out for the change in the FL/GDP ratio. The explanation is that the increase in FL/GDP ratio is a result of acceleration of the foreign capital inflow in response to a decrease in foreign economic growth and consequently in demand for the Czech export (a decrease in NX/GDP ratio), which may imply a decrease in EUR reference rate and subsequently in CZK reference rate.

Table 3. Results of the econometric model estimation

Eq.	Y_t	C (t-stat.)	Y_{t-y} α_y (t-stat.)	$B_{1,t-x}$ $\beta_{1,t-x}$ (t-stat.)	$B_{2,t-x}$ $\beta_{2,t-x}$ (t-stat.)	$B_{3,t-x}$ $\beta_{3,t-x}$ (t-stat.)	$B_{4,t-x}$ $\beta_{4,t-x}$ (t-stat.)	Adj. R^2
1	$\Delta\frac{NX_t}{GDP_t}$	-	t-1 0,718* (6,659)	ΔIR^{EUR}_{t-6} 0,279* (2,798)	$\Delta\gamma_{t-7}$ -0,118** (-1,953)	-	-	0,47
2	$\Delta\gamma_t$	-	t-1 0,822* (7,990) t-3 -0,361* (-3,557) t-5 -0,490** (-2,304)	ΔIR^{CZK}_{t-5} -0,490* (-2,304)	er_{t-1} -0,045*** (-1,829)	-	-	0,68
3	Δir^{FL}_t	-	t-1 -0,492* (-4,419)	ΔIR^{CZK}_{t-2} 0,456*** (1,880)	$\Delta\gamma_{t-8}$ -0,224** (-1,962)	$\Delta\frac{NX_{t-1}}{GDP_{t-1}}$ 0,367*** (1,688)	$\Delta\frac{FL_{T-5}}{GDP_{t-5}}$ -0,169* (-3,232)	0,52
4	er_t	-0,013* (-3,406)	t-3 -0,233*** (-1.829)	$\Delta\frac{FA_T}{GDP_t}$ 0,678* (3,718)	$\Delta\gamma_{t-3}$ -0,902** (-2,083)	-	-	0,40
5	Δrp^{FL}_t	-	t-4 -0,498* (-3,913)	div^{FL}_t -0,047* (-2,595)	$\Delta\gamma_{t-6}$ -0,591* (-3,392)	$\Delta\frac{NX_{t-1}}{GDP_{t-1}}$ 0,834** (2,186)	-	0,35
6	div^{FL}_t	0,060* (5,510)	-	$\Delta\gamma_{t-5}$ -1,017*** (-1,593)	Dummy1 -0,046* (-2,924)	Dummy2 0,033** (2,193)	Dummy3 0,034** (2,244)	0,44
7	$\Delta\frac{FL_T}{GDP_t}$	0,007* (2,489)	t-3 -0,488* (-4,390)	Δir^{FL}_t 0,319*** (1,929)	div^{FL}_t 0,133* (4,096)	$\Delta\frac{NX_{t-2}}{GDP_{t-2}}$ 1,017* (2,636)	er_{t-3} 0,145* (2,559)	0,50

*, **, *** - significant at 1%, 5% a 10% level, Dummy1, dummy2 and dummy3 – dummy variables for the 1st, 2nd and 3rd quarter.

Source: my own calculations.

If the faster foreign capital inflow did not directly result from decreasing export performance of the Czech economy, an increase in FL/GDP ratio should cause the faster appreciation of Czech crown. However, equation 4 does not confirm that FL/GDP has a statistically significant impact on exchange rate dynamics, instead, it shows that there exists a relatively strong influence of the change in FA/GDP ratio on exchange rate, i.e. the acceleration of foreign capital outflow from domestic economy causes the faster depreciation (slower appreciation) of Czech crown. Besides, exchange rate is very strongly influenced by the economic growth rate (with a lag of three quarters of the year) when the growth rate deceleration causes the almost identical counteractive reaction of Czech crown exchange rate. This is a very unpleasant scenario for the Czech economy because at the time of crisis it deepens its negative NFA, increases the costs paid from NFA, and moreover, weakens the economy performance and worsens the dynamics of NFA/GDP ratio.

The analysis of the costs paid from property liabilities confirms the existence of a weaker counteractive relationship between changes in reinvested profits and the size of dividend yield of liabilities (equation 6). The lower intensity is apparently a consequence of the fact that both types of costs are compensated as late as at the end of the period in connection with financial crisis and growth slump in other countries. Both in dividend yield (equation 5) and in changes in reinvested profit, the deceleration of economic growth surprisingly increases their values (lag of five and sex quarters of the year, resp.), which does not prove the influence of domestic demand dynamics on the profitability ratios of direct foreign investments in the CR. On the contrary, a significant export nature of these property investments is confirmed because estimations record a strong positive relation of reinvested profit with changes in NX/GDP ratio with a lag of one quarter of the year. This relation should theoretically reduce the amount of costs paid from foreign liabilities, however, there is a problem of the non-existence of any relationship between changes in reinvested profit and in dividend yield of foreign liabilities after adjustment for its strong seasonal variation.

Ultimately, changes in FL/GDP ratio are a function of the costs paid by domestic firms to foreign investors and a function of changes in the Czech crown exchange rate and changes in NX/GDP ratio (equation 7). Obviously, changes in foreign capital inflow respond especially to changes in dividend and interest rate costs of foreign liabilities (without lag). Exchange rate changes have a weaker positive influence (a lag of three quarters of the year), but the Czech crown depreciation does not have a fatal influence on changes in

FL/GDP ratio. The positive influence of changes in NX/GDP seems to be extraordinarily strong. It confirms again the export nature of domestic firms owned by foreign investors when the increase in NX/GDP ratio is connected in the first phase with the inflow of debt foreign capital providing the operational financing of export while debt financing subsequently turns into the foreign investor's reinvested profit. It implies a certain risk because increases in net export creating resources for the financing of NFA costs automatically generate foreign liabilities and resulting costs further deepen the negative NFA position.

CONCLUSION

The basic concept of negative NFA sustainability is presented that is based on a comparison of resources the economy is able to produce mainly by positive output balance and of particular forms of net costs of servicing the negative NFA position. Obviously, it is justified to expect that transition economies have to pay relatively high costs of servicing the negative NFA position compared to developed economies. These costs result from the position of transition economies as net recipients of foreign investments and their high dividend costs and costs of reinvested profit. Besides, a high share of low-yielding foreign exchange reserves of central bank in the country's foreign assets plays its role. It is also to assume that these countries cannot denominate foreign liabilities in domestic currency to a larger extent and so they cannot influence the costs of foreign debt liabilities in this way. On the contrary, as a result of the positive interest rate differential between domestic and foreign credit market the position of foreign currency credits on the side of foreign liabilities is many times escalated with potentially negative impacts on the stability of their recipients in the case of domestic currency depreciation. Therefore it is rather difficult for transition economies to reach the condition of NFA sustainability in the long run and to decrease the ratio of NFA in GDP, which is one of the frequent criteria of robustness of the economic development of a given country.

The empirical analysis on an example of the CR in 2000-2011 demonstrates the relatively high levels of costs paid from the negative CR NFA (particularly on the side of dividend and interest yields) that exceed the resources domestic economy generates within surplus output balance and balance of transfers and returns on labour. Besides, domestic economy is not able to fulfil the condition of NFA sustainability in the long run and mostly not even in the short run. It is to note that the long-term trends of particular variables in the condition of sustainability show quite different characteristics in comparison with mutual relations in the short run. These relations mostly confirm a number of positive trends, e.g. an increase in the economy's capacity to generate resources in the situation of an increase in the costs paid from NFA, anti-cyclic behaviour of NFA/GDP ratio in relation to foreign demand and endogeneity of the interest yield of foreign liabilities. On the contrary, it is clearly confirmed that the worsening ratio of NFA/GDP and/or FL/GDP is a result of high dividend costs paid from foreign property liabilities, the first differences of which are negatively related to a change in foreign demand for domestic export, and last but not least, the strong counteractive reaction of CZK/EUR exchange rate appears as significant if a change in the economic growth rate occurs. Ultimately, the worsening of the NFA/GDP ratio of Czech economy does not pose a problem from foreign investors' aspect that would complicate the inflow of (re)financing capital; however, in the context of the present difficult situation under debt crisis it would be more than beneficial if domestic economy at least stabilized the negative ratio of NFA/GDP and fulfilled the sustainability condition in the short run.

References

Brůna, K., Durčáková, J. (2012): Banking system liquidity absorption and monetary base backing in the context of exchange rate policy in the Czech Republic, Poland and Hungary. *Post-Communist Economies*, 2012, Vol. 24, No. 2, p. 257–275.

Freund, C. (2000): Current Account Adjustments in Industrialized Countries. *International Finance Discussion Papers*, 2000, No. 692, p. 1-31.

Ghironi, F., İscan, T.B., Rebucci, A. (2005): Net Foreign Asset Position and Consumption Dynamics in the International Economy. Washington: International Monetary Fund, *IMF Working Paper*, 2005, WP/05/82.

Gourinchas, P. O. Rey, H. (2005): International Financial Adjustment. Cambridge: National Bureau of Economic Research, NBER Working Paper Series, 2005, No. 11155.

Higgins, M., Klitgaard, T., TILLE, C. (2005): The Income Implications of Rising U.S. International Liabilities. *Current Issues in Economics and Finance*, 2005, Vol. 11, No. 12, p. 1-9.

Higgins, M., Klitgaard, (2005): Financial Globalization and the U.S. Current Account Deficit. *Current Issues in Economics and Finance*, 2007, Vol. 13, No. 11, p. 1-7.

Lane, P. R., Milesi-Ferretti, G. M. (2003): International Financial Integration. Dublin: Institute for International Integration Studies, IIIS Discussion Paper, No. 3, 2003.

Lane, P. R., Milesi-Ferretti, G. M. (2002): Long-Term Capital Movements. *NBER Macroeconomics Annual*, 2001, Vol. 16, p. 73-136.

Mandel, M., Tomšík, V. (2008): External Balance in a Transition Economy. *Eastern European Economics*, Vol. 46, No. 4, 2008, p. 5-26.

Sandri, D. (2011): Precautionary Savings and Global Imbalances in World General Equilibrium. Washington: International Monetary Fund, IMF Working Paper, 2011, WP/11/122.

Summers, L. (2006): Reflections on Global Account Imbalances and Emerging Markets Reserve Accumulation. L. K. *Jha Memorial Lecture,* 2006, Reserve Bank of India.

Tille, C. (2003): The Impact of Exchange Rate Movements on U.S. Foreign Debt. *Current Issues in Economics and Finance,* 2003, Vol. 9, No. 1, p. 1-7.

In: Macroeconomics
Editor: Carly M. Hutson

ISBN: 978-1-63463-596-7

Chapter 2

THE MEESE-ROGOFF PUZZLE: WHAT PUZZLE?

Imad A. Moosa[1,*] and Kelly Burns[2]
[1]RMIT, Melbourne VIC, Australia
[2]Curtin University, Bentley WA, Australia

ABSTRACT

The Messe-Rogoff puzzle has been a debatable topic since 1983 when Richard Meese and Kenneth Rogoff demonstrated that no exchange rate model can outperform the random walk in out-of-sample forecasting. This finding been taken to imply the weakness of international economics and finance and raised the question as to why firms spend money on exchange rate forecasts and use them as an input in the financial decision making process when these forecasts are inferior to those of the random walk. In this chapter we resolve the puzzle by reaching the following conclusions: (i) we should expect nothing but that exchange rate models cannot outperform the random walk in out-of-sample forecasting if forecasting accuracy is measured by metrics that depend on the magnitude of the forecasting error only; (ii) the use of dynamic models to outperform the random walk is inappropriate because it is tantamount to beating a random walk with a random walk; and (iii) it is possible to outperform the random walk in terms of other metrics such as direction accuracy and profitability.

* Corresponding author: Imad A. Moosa. School of Economics, Finance and Marketing, RMIT, 445 Swanston Street, Melbourne, Victoria 3000, Australia.

INTRODUCTION

In what has become a frequently cited paper, Meese and Rogoff (1983) demonstrated that exchange rate models cannot outperform the random walk in out-of-sample forecasting. The Meese-Rogoff results stimulated significant research, and numerous attempts have been made to overturn their findings by using a variety of data, sample periods, methodologies and model specifications. Most of these attempts have been "unsuccessful", in the sense that the Meese-Rogoff results could not be overturned. Some economists, however, have claimed victory over the random walk (by producing numerically smaller forecasting errors), but they failed to conduct formal testing and opted instead to derive inference on the basis of the numerical values of measures of forecasting accuracy (which is easy and convenient but deceptive). Otherwise, they (the "victors") used dynamic models, which boils down to beating the random walk with a random walk augmented with explanatory variables. Although a minority of economists attempted to and succeeded in resolving the puzzle by using alternative measures of forecasting accuracy, they undermined the significance of their work by not claiming that their results overturned the Meese-Rogoff conclusion. This strand of research is a manifestation of confirmation bias (confirmation of the Meese-Rogoff results) and the fear of challenging the status quo.

The Meese-Rogoff results are viewed as a puzzle because it makes no sense for profit-maximizing firms to spend money on professional forecasts when the random walk provides free and "more accurate" forecasts. The puzzle is allegedly a disgrace to the profession because the enormous amount of work that has been done in the field of exchange rate economics has not led to the formulation of a model that is better than the (naive) random walk. Believing that there is a puzzle, economists have put forward several explanations for the Meese-Rogoff findings.

Meese and Rogoff themselves explained the puzzle in terms of some econometric problems, including simultaneous equations bias, sampling errors, stochastic movements in the true underlying parameters, model misspecification, the failure to account for non-linearities, and the proxies used for inflationary expectations. However, the main reason underpinning, and the root cause of, the Meese-Rogoff puzzle has been overlooked in the literature. Assessing forecasting accuracy exclusively by the magnitude of the forecasting error (which is what Meese and Rogoff did) is the only explanation as to why the random walk cannot be outperformed.

In fact, we should expect nothing other than the failure of exchange rate models to produce numerically (let alone statistically) smaller forecasting errors than the random walk.

In this chapter we attempt to resolve the Meese-Rogoff puzzle by utilizing a wider range of forecasting accuracy measures that do not rely exclusively on the magnitude of the forecasting error. We demonstrate that exchange rate models can outperform the random walk in out-of-sample forecasting when forecasting accuracy is assessed by measures that take into account more than just the magnitude of the forecasting error. We also demonstrate that other explanations, such as those suggested by Meese and Rogoff themselves, cannot resolve the puzzle. For this purpose, some empirical results are presented based on one of the models used by Meese and Rogoff, the Frenkel-Bilson flexible-price monetary model. The Dornbusch-Frankel sticky-price monetary model is used only when we examine inflationary expectations. The models are estimated for six exchange rates involving the US dollar (USD), Japanese yen (JPY), British pound (GBP), Canadian dollar (CAD) and Australian dollar (AUD). The estimation is based on monthly data covering the period January 1984-June 2001, while (one-month ahead) forecasts are generated over the period July 2001-June 2011.

THE MEESE-ROGOFF RESULTS AND THE AFTERMATH

In the original study that triggered the controversy, Meese and Rogoff (1983) used three exchange rate models: the Frenkel-Bilson (F-B) flexible-price monetary model, the Dornbusch-Frankel (D-F) sticky-price monetary model and the Hooper-Morton (H-M) sticky-price monetary model incorporating current account effects. They estimated the models by using monthly data spanning the period 1973 to 1981 for three bilateral exchange rates (the US dollar against the German mark, Japanese yen and British pound). By comparing the numerical values of the forecasting errors (measured using the mean absolute error, mean square error and root mean square error), Meese and Rogoff concluded that the random walk could not be outperformed in exchange rate forecasting. Despite the enormous amount of research that has been conducted since the publication of the Meese and Rogoff results, failure to outperform the random walk has been accepted at face value and considered an undisputed fact of life.

The Meese-Rogoff results have been re-examined over and over again since 1983 because they are interpreted to imply a serious weakness in the field of international monetary economics and finance. For example, Abhyankar et al. (2005) describe the Meese-Rogoff findings as a "major puzzle in international finance". Evans and Lyons (2004, 2005) contend that the Meese-Rogoff finding "has proven robust over the decades" despite it being "the most researched puzzle in international macroeconomics". Fair (2008) describes exchange rate models as "not the pride of open economy macroeconomics" and asserts that the "general view still seems pessimistic". Engel et al. (2007) summarize the current state of affairs by stating that the "explanatory power of these models is essentially zero". Frankel and Rose (1995) argue that the "puzzle" has a "pessimistic effect" on the field of exchange rate modelling in particular and international finance in general. Bacchetta and van Wincoop (2006) describe the "puzzle" as most likely the major weakness of international macroeconomics. Neely and Sarno (2002) consider the Meese and Rogoff conclusion to be a "devastating critique" of the monetary approach to exchange rate determination and to have "marked a watershed in exchange rate economics". Flood and Rose (2008) emphasize the point that the Meese-Rogoff results are "devastating for the field of international finance", going as far as claiming that "the area [international finance] has fell into disrepute" and that "the area is not even represented on many first-rate academic faculties"!! Thus there is an apparent bewilderment as to why exchange rate models cannot outperform the random walk, leading to dramatic claims about the miserable state of international finance, which allegedly has fallen into disrepute. These claims are gross overstatements and represent an unnecessary dramatization of the current state of affairs. If the field is in a bad shape, it is not because no model can outperform the random walk but rather because the Meese-Rogoff puzzle has been allowed to survive for such a long time.

The Meese-Rogoff paper exhibits several flaws. For one thing they fail to test the statistical significance of the difference between measures of forecasting accuracy and instead derive inference on the basis of the numerical values of those measures. They used, as measures of forecasting accuracy, metrics that are based on the magnitude of the forecasting error although predicting the direction of change is more important for the profitability of trading. They also used the lagged forward rate as a forecaster and the lagged spot rate as a benchmark, which makes no sense whatsoever. Last, but not least, Meese and Rogoff corrected for serial correlation and used rolling regressions to generate out-of-sample forecasts. Serial correlation implies model misspecification, in which case the model should be re-specified rather than dealing with the symptom by wiping out serial correlation. Using rolling as opposed to recursive regressions to generate forecasts amounts to a deliberate loss of information. More important, however, is that the random walk is a nonsensical and dumb forecasting model, which means that it takes a big suspension of disbelief to accept the Meese-Rogoff results (and their faulty interpretation) at face value.

Studies that have been conducted to resolve the Meese-Rogoff puzzle may be classified into one of the three categories. In the first category are "copycats" that follow the Meese-Rogoff methodology, making the same mistakes, obtaining similar results and preserving the myth of the puzzle. In the second category are those that claim victory over the random walk by using econometric modifications such as the introduction of dynamics and non-linearities and by using time-varying parametric (TVP) estimation. The authors of category two studies typically derive inference without appropriate testing. Those who conduct proper testing and reach the conclusion that their models outperform the random walk do so by using dynamic modelling, which effectively boils down to beating the random walk with a random walk. Category three comprises studies that preserve the myth of the puzzle by overlooking the fact that beating the random walk does not necessarily mean producing lower forecasting errors, which means that attention is diverted away from the root cause of the puzzle (that is, improper measures of forecasting accuracy). With a few exceptions (for example, Moosa and Burns, 2013a, 2014a), no study dismisses the Meese-Rogoff results (because they are flawed) and consequently suggests an explanation for the puzzle.

It is no wonder that the Meese-Rogoff puzzle has survived the test of time. In the remainder of this chapter we examine each of the explanations suggested in the literature and explore the possibility of resolving the puzzle by introducing the necessary modifications to the models and procedures used by Meese and Rogoff. We will show that the only way to outperform the random walk is to use alternative measures of forecasting accuracy to those used by Meese and Rogoff. Eventually we will discard the Meese-Rogoff puzzle as a myth. This task is executed by presenting a series of propositions.

Proposition 1: A Natural Outcome, Not a Puzzle

The inability of exchange rate models to outperform the random walk by producing smaller forecasting errors is a natural outcome, not a puzzle. We should expect nothing but that exchange rate models cannot outperform the random walk in terms of the magnitude of the forecasting error, particularly over short forecasting horizons and when high-frequency data are used. Kilian and Taylor (2003) raise the question as to why it is so difficult to beat the random walk in the title of their paper, a question that can be answered intuitively. Engel (1994) argues that beating the random walk in terms of the magnitude of error is not an appropriate benchmark because it always produces small errors, making it difficult (if not impossible) to beat on this basis. They go on to suggest that beating the random walk in terms of the root mean square error (RMSE) is "too strong a criterion for accepting a model".

If the underlying exchange rate (or any financial price) is relatively stable, the forecasting error of the random walk will be small. As the exchange rate becomes more volatile, the forecasting error of the random walk grows bigger. At the same time, however, the forecasting error produced by any model grows bigger as well. Thus, if we start from a situation of a stable exchange rate where the forecasting error of the random walk is smaller than that of the model, then as long as the error of the random walk does not grow faster than that of the model, the model will always produce a larger root mean square error. This observation is equally valid for other financial prices such as stock prices.

Some empirical evidence is available to support this proposition. By using simulated data to account for a wide range of volatility, Moosa (2013) demonstrates that as volatility rises, the forecasting error of any model rises more rapidly than that of the random walk. Likewise, Moosa and Vaz (2014) demonstrate, by using two stock price models, that as price volatility rises, the RMSE of the random walk rises but the RMSE of the model rises more rapidly. It follows that the Meese-Rogoff finding is a natural outcome, not a puzzle, and that nothing is remarkable about their results. As the period-to-period change in the exchange rate is typically small (which is by definition the magnitude of the error of the random walk), the random walk will always produce a comparatively smaller RMSE, making it almost impossible for the exchange rate model to generate a numerically smaller and statistically different RMSE. This should not mean that the random walk is good and exchange rate models are bad, because what matters is not only the numerical value of the magnitude of the forecasting error.

Proposition 2: The Random Walk Is a Dumb Model

The random walk is a dumb model, which means that it should not be difficult to outperform by using appropriate measures of forecasting accuracy.

The reason why it is dumb is that the random walk produces forecasts that follow and turn after the actual values—hence the actual values forecast the forecast values. Intuitively, we should expect any model to outperform a dumb model like the random walk because the random walk without drift tells us that the period-to-period change in the exchange rate is zero while the random walk with drift implies that the exchange rate always rises or falls. These predictions are the inconsistent with the observed behavior of exchange rates.

Intuitively we should expect any model to outperform the random walk in terms of direction accuracy because exchange rates do change and do not fall or rise persistently. The random walk (in a stochastic form) conveys a plausible idea that the exchange rate is as likely to rise as to fall, but using it (in a deterministic form) as a benchmark to measure forecasting accuracy is not the right thing to do. This is why the random walk is justifiably dubbed "naive" and "dumb", which makes us wonder why it is used as a benchmark in the first place.

Proposition 3: The Forward Rate As a Forecaster

It is inappropriate, even flawed, to use the lagged forward rate as a forecaster and the lagged spot rate as a benchmark. The lagged forward rate (which Meese and Rogoff used as forecaster) performs equally badly in forecasting exchange rates as the lagged spot rate (implied by the random walk). Both of these bad forecasters fall under the so-called "market-based forecasting", implying that (good-quality) forecasts can be obtained for free (Moosa, 2004a). The forward rate is not a good forecaster of the future spot rate because the two rates are determined simultaneously via covered interest parity (CIP). The forward rate is calculated by adjusting the spot rate for a factor that reflects the interest rate differential. Since the two rates are related contemporaneously, the lagged exchange rate (the forecaster) turns after the actual rate (the "forecastee"). Market-based forecasting, whereby the market provides the forecasts (the lagged spot and forward rates) free of charge, is naive because it is based on the two naive ideas that the exchange rate either does not change (the random walk) or that it is equal to the lagged forward rate (the unbiased efficiency hypothesis). In finance there is no free lunch, where "lunch" in this case refers to the ability to make risk-free profit. Using the lagged forward rate as a forecaster and the random walk as a benchmark is inappropriate (to say the least) because the lagged spot and forward rates are almost perfectly correlated and not independent.

Moosa and Burns (2014c) provide evidence to support this proposition by calculating the RMSEs of the forecasts generated by the lagged spot (i.e. random walk model) and forward rates for four currency combinations. The results show that the RMSEs are not only insignificantly different from each other but also that they are numerically identical. One might as well use the lagged forward rate as a benchmark. It remains to say that the spot and forward rates are not independent because they are linked via a contemporaneous relation (CIP) that precludes profitable arbitrage and allows the hedging of a forward position (see, for example, Moosa, 2004b).

Proposition 4: The Use of Magnitude-Only Criteria

The Meese-Rogoff results cannot be overturned by using magnitude-only measures of forecasting accuracy such as the root mean square error. Meese and Rogoff used three, magnitude-only, measures of forecasting accuracy: mean error, mean absolute error and mean square error (hence the root mean square error). To start with, the mean error is so misleading that a very poor forecasting model may appear as if it generates perfect forecasts if the negative and positive errors cancel out, producing a zero mean error. It is because this metric is so misleading that preference is given to the mean absolute error (MAE) and mean square error (MSE), whereby the problem associated with the mean error is circumvented by averaging absolute errors and squared errors, respectively. Although Flood and Rose (2008) believe that the mean error is misleading, they use it only because Meese and Rogoff did. In this sense the Meese-Rogoff paper is influential as it is followed blindly and with hardly any scrutiny. Flood and Rose, and others, overlook the fact that all of these measures are misleading in another sense, because they only take into account the magnitude of the error.

Using the data described earlier we generate out-of-sample (one-month-ahead) forecasts from the Frenkel-Bilson model. In Figure 1 we observe the root mean square errors (where the forecasting error is calculated as a fraction of the actual value) of the random walk and the model for six exchange rates. In no case does the model produce a numerically smaller RMSE than that of the random walk. This is a natural outcome as we argued under proposition 1. But this does not mean that the random walk is not a dumb forecaster as we argued under proposition 2. Studies show that changing the forecasting horizon or the model does not make much difference to these results (for example, Moosa and Burns, 2013a, 2014a, 2014c).

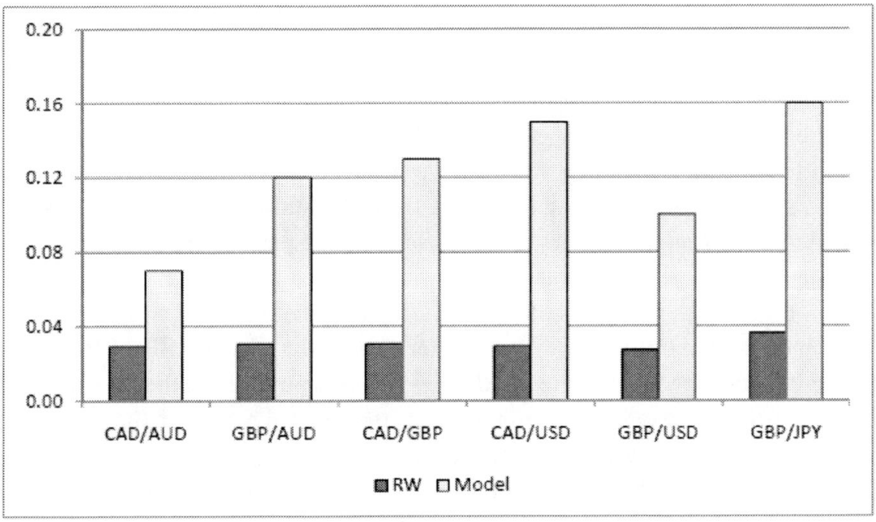

Figure 1. RMSEs of the Random Walk and the Static Frenkel-Bilson Model.

Proposition 5: Hypothesis Testing Is Imperative

Judging the superiority or otherwise of the model over the random walk should be based on hypothesis testing as applied to the difference between forecasting errors. In empirical work, applied economists typically test for the difference between means, variances, ratios, etc. This is because these statistics are not deterministic quantities—rather, they are estimated with standard errors, which means that the numerical values on their own are inadequate for the purpose of deriving inference. To find out if a model produces a forecasting error that is lower or higher than that of the random walk, we must determine (by appropriate testing) whether or not the difference is statistically significant. If the root mean square error of a model is, say, 3.45 percent and that of the random walk is 3.50 percent, can we conclude that the model is superior to the random walk? In general, can we derive inference on the basis of a numerical comparison of quantitative measures of forecasting accuracy? The answer to both of these two questions is a definite no. Yet this is exactly what Meese and Rogoff did (or did not do).

Most subsequent studies made the same mistake, but some of them correctly used the Diebold-Mariano (1995) test without emphasizing the point that Meese and Rogoff failed to do that, and hence their (Meese and Rogoff's) results could not be taken seriously.

Meese and Rogoff should not be excused for failing to do that because the Diebold-Mariano test was not available in the early 1980s when they carried out their work.

The AGS test of Ashley et al. (1980) was available then, which makes it natural to speculate that they were not aware of the existence of this test. Even if no test is available, deriving inference from the numerical values of statistics estimated with standard errors is not exactly right, particularly in a paper that has received so much attention.

In Figure 2 we present the AGS test statistics for six currency combinations. The null hypothesis in this case is that the RMSE of the model is equal to the RMSE of the random walk. The null hypothesis cannot be rejected if the test statistic is smaller than the critical value of the chi-square distribution with two degrees of freedom.

We can see that the test statistics are massive and exceed any critical value even at the 1 or 0.5 percent level of significance. This means that in all cases the random walk is superior to the random walk.

Any inference on the magnitude of the RMSEs should be based on a test like this. The results presented in Figure 2 confirm that the model cannot outperform the random walk in out-of-sample forecasting in terms of the root mean square error. This finding confirms the Meese-Rogoff results.

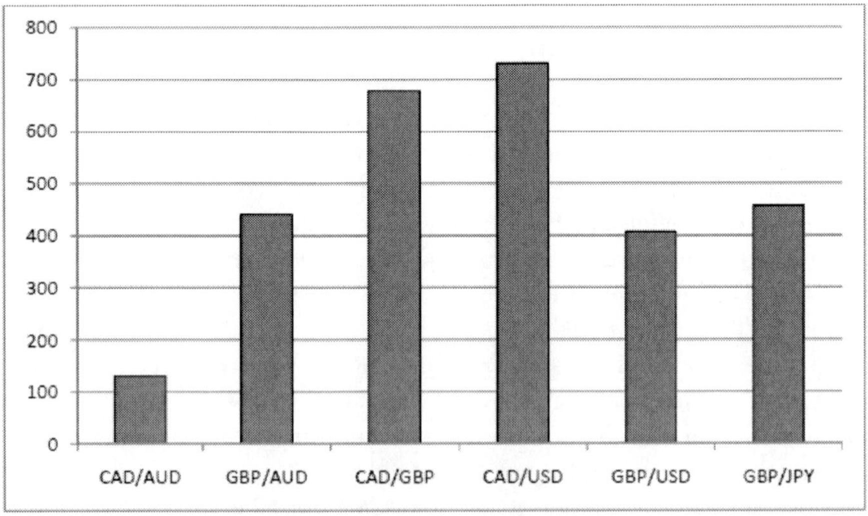

Figure 2. AGS Test Statistics—Static Frenkel-Bilson Model.

Proposition 6: The Use of Alternative Criteria

The Meese-Rogoff results cannot be overturned except by using alternative measures of forecasting accuracy. Several economists have suggested the use of alternative measures of forecasting accuracy and managed to outperform the random walk, but no one presented their findings as an explanation for the puzzle, thus perpetuating the myth of the puzzle.

Relying on magnitude-only measures of forecasting accuracy is not always appropriate, and a consensus is emerging that criteria other than just magnitude should be used (Engel and Hamilton, 1990; Cheung et al., 2005; Moosa and Burns, 2012, 2013a, 2013b, 2014a).

Alternative criteria include direction accuracy (Engel and Hamilton, 1990; Cheung et al., 2005; Moosa and Burns, 2012), profitability (Leitch and Tanner, 1991; Li, 2011; Moosa and Burns, 2012, 2013a, 2014a), proximity to a perfect forecast (Moosa and Burns, 2013b), and the adjusted root mean square error (ARMSE) (Moosa and Burns, 2012).

Cheung et al. (2005) argue that using criteria other than the mean square error does not boil down to "changing the rules of the game". They advocate the use of other criteria because minimizing the MSE may not be important from an economic standpoint and that it may miss out on important aspects of prediction, particularly at long horizons.

Christoffersen and Diebold (1998) point out that the MSE indicates no improvement in predictions that take into account cointegrating relation *vis-à-vis* univariate prediction. Faust et al. (2003) argue that "the absence of statistically significant predictive power need not indicate that an optimal decision-maker should ignore the model", citing optimal investment strategies as an important example. Unfortunately, the arguments put forward by Christoffersen and Diebold (1998) and Faust et al. (2003) are irrelevant or ambiguous, respectively. The presence or absence of cointegration does not make a systematic difference for the forecasting accuracy of the underlying model—at least no evidence is provided to support this proposition. It is not that the MSE is no good because it indicates no improvement in predictions that take into account the presence of cointegration but rather because it only takes into account the magnitude of the forecasting error.

Moosa (2006) suggests that forecasting accuracy should be defined and measured depending on the underlying decision rule. Corte et al. (2009) correctly attribute failure to beat the random walk to the use of improper criteria that do not take into account the real economic gains produced by the forecasts (that is, in terms of profitability).

Neely and Sarno (2002) conclude that "the literature on exchange rate forecasting has shown that the amount of exchange rate variations explained by monetary models is – at most – small", but that the conclusions one draws "depend on the purpose of these forecasting exercises, which is little discussed in the literature". Moosa (2000) points out that the most important consideration when exchange rate forecasts are assessed is whether or not they lead to sound decisions. It is the purpose of exchange rate forecasting that influences the method of evaluation and the conclusions reached about relative forecasting superiority (Neely and Sarno, 2002).

Under some circumstances, the direction of change is the only criterion of importance when assessing forecasting accuracy. Engel (1994) suggests that this observation is valid in the case of a central bank under a pegged exchange rate system where intervention is required if the currency is expected to depreciate, "regardless of the size of the expected depreciation". Moosa (2006) suggests intraday trading, where the interest rate factor is negligible, as another example of when direction accuracy is the only important criterion. Several studies have unquestionably demonstrated that the random walk can be outperformed by exchange rate models in terms of direction of change, despite its superiority in terms of the magnitude of change. While Engel (1994) finds that a Markov-switching model cannot outperform the random walk in terms of the magnitude of the error, he provides evidence indicating that the model is superior in predicting the direction of change in the exchange rate. Likewise, Moosa and Burns (2013a) show that when forecasting power is judged by direction accuracy, the Meese-Rogoff puzzle can be resolved, providing evidence to indicate that exchange rate models have direction accuracy that is numerically higher and statistically different from zero, and often exceeds 50 percent.

There is a growing body of literature that promotes profitability as the ultimate test or measure of forecasting power (for example, Leitch and Tanner, 1991; Moosa and Burns, 2013a). Consideration of profitability resolves the anomaly observed by Leitch and Tanner (1991) that economists are puzzled as to why profit-maximizing firms pay for professional forecasts when conventional forecasting accuracy measures show that the random walk provides superior (and free) forecasts. Indeed the literature supports the superiority of models over the random walk when profitability is used to assess forecasting performance. Abhyankar et al. (2005) find that the relative performance of exchange rate models improves when a utility-based criterion is used. They consider the realized wealth from using macroeconomic forecasts to determine optimal weights in a diversified portfolio of foreign and domestic assets and find evidence for the inferiority of the random walk. Likewise, West et al. (1993) suggest a utility-based evaluation of exchange rate predictability, where utility in this context is measured by profitability. Li (2011) finds that the profitability of carry trade and risk-return measures can be enhanced by using forecasts.

Moosa and Burns (2012) propose a measure of forecasting accuracy (the adjusted root mean square error, ARMSE) that takes into account both magnitude and direction accuracy without bias to either. The ARMSE is calculated by adjusting the RMSE for direction accuracy, which means that for two models with the same RMSE, the one with the better direction accuracy will have a lower ARMSE. They also propose a test for proximity to a perfect forecast as a means to evaluate both magnitude and direction accuracy in a single measure (Moosa and Burns, 2013b). The test involves the running of a regression of predicted change on actual change, followed by the use of a Wald test for the joint coefficient restriction to determine the proximity of the forecasts to the line of perfect forecast (represented by a 45-degree line on a prediction-realisation diagram). Since the numerical value of the test statistic (which has a χ^2 distribution) is indicative of the deviation of the intercept and slope from 0 and 1 respectively, it is possible to determine which of two or more models generates forecasts that are closer to a perfect forecast by comparing the values of the Wald test statistic. Moosa and Burns (2013b) use this test to evaluate forecasts of the flexible-price monetary model and random walk and find that the values of the χ^2 statistic for the random walk are multiples of those associated with the monetary model. This means that the deviation of the model forecasts from the line of perfect forecast is smaller than that of (hence the model is better than) the random walk. While conventional macroeconomic models are not that good in the traditional sense, they provide better (or less bad) forecasts than the random walk when the direction of change is taken into account.

Proposition 6 is supported by the results presented in Figure 3, which reports direction accuracy, the ARMSE, mean return and proximity to a perfect forecast for the Frenkel-Bilson model *vis-a-vis* the random walk. Direction accuracy takes values between zero and one. Since the random walk without drift predicts no change while exchange rates typically change, it has a direction accuracy of zero. The model, however, produces direction accuracy of over 0.60 for the CAD/AUD. In all cases, the null hypothesis that direction accuracy is zero is rejected, implying that the model is superior to the random walk in terms of direction accuracy.

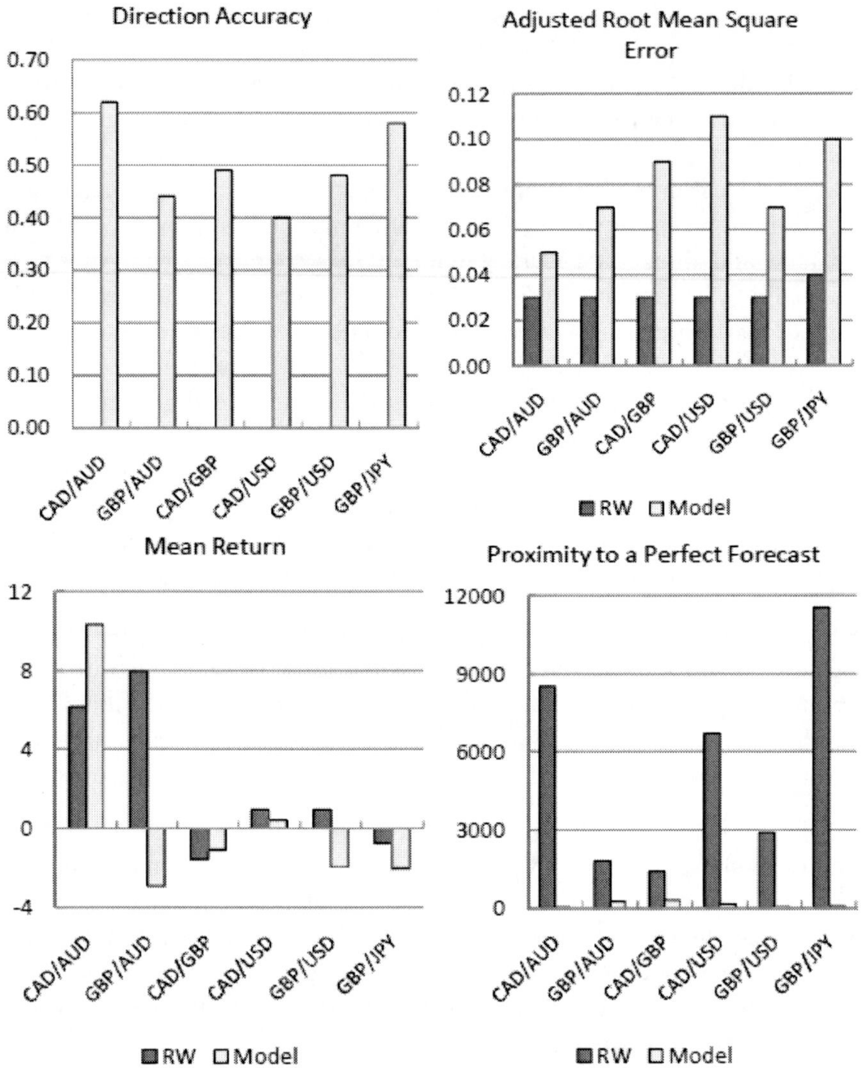

Figure 3. Alternative Measures of Forecasting Accuracy—Static Frenkel-Bilson Model.

Despite this finding, the random walk outperforms the model in terms of the ARMSE because the random walk is so superior in terms of the magnitude of error.

The mean return is that of a trading strategy that incorporates the generated forecasts whereas the mean return for the random walk is that derived from carry trade (assuming no change in the exchange rate).

In two out of four cases the model outperforms the random walk, which means that there is some value in the forecasts, and helps explain why profit maximizing firms pay for professional forecasts rather than relying on the random walk forecasts. As for proximity to a perfect forecast, the model is far superior to the random walk in all cases. As we can see, the value of the test statistic for the random walk is massive in all cases, implying huge deviation from the line of perfect forecast.

Proposition 7: TVP Estimation

The Meese-Rogoff results cannot be overturned by using time-varying parametric (TVP) estimation. Meese and Rogoff (1983) suggested that a possible reason for the failure of exchange rate models to outperform the random walk is the use of constant rather than time-varying parameters. A review of the literature suggests that estimating exchange rate models in a TVP framework may enhance forecasting performance, but whether or not the improvement (if any) is sufficient to outperform the random walk and resolve the Meese-Rogoff puzzle is a different matter.

Schinasi and Swamy (1989) advocate the use of TVP estimation of exchange rate models for a number of reasons. First, model parameters may change over time because traders do not use information in the same way over all policy regimes and across all time horizons. Second, market participants are heterogeneous, which means that macroeconomic variables are not related to the exchange rate by a simple fixed-coefficient relation. Third, the use of fixed coefficients implies the imposition of a restriction that may or may not hold. Fourth, the empirical evidence suggests that the fixed-coefficient restrictions may not be valid in macroeconomic models.

Several other studies have shown that, depending on current economic conditions, the same macroeconomic fundamentals can play a different role in the monetary model. Junttila and Korhonen (2011), for example, show that the significance of the coefficients on the explanatory variables may differ, according to the monetary regime, and consequently the sample chosen for the forecasting exercise. They find that the coefficient on relative interest rates has similar magnitudes, but different signs, depending on the current regime. Based on their results, they conclude that fundamentals play different roles in the monetary model under different inflationary conditions. Likewise, Wolff (1987) suggests that parameter instability in exchange rate models may arise from instability in the money demand function, policy regime shifts, and changes in the long-run real exchange rate (emanating from changes in oil prices or global trade patterns). Frommel et al. (2005) provide evidence for the presence of an unstable and non-linear relation between fundamentals and exchange rates. They demonstrate that the impact of macroeconomic variables (such as short-term interest rates, inflation differentials and economic growth) on the exchange rate is closely related to the monetary policy regime and regime switches.

Following Schinasi and Swamy (1989), Moosa and Burns (2013a) replicate the Meese-Rogoff study by using the same exchange rates and time period but they estimate the models in a TVP framework. The results demonstrate that the Meese and Rogoff findings cannot be overturned, even if the models are estimated with time-varying parameters, in the sense that the TVP models cannot outperform the random walk in terms of the magnitude of the forecasting error. Unlike Schinasi and Swamy (1989), Moosa and Burns (2013a) use the AGS test to reach this conclusion. This finding is consistent with that of Rossi (2006) in that TVP estimation of exchange rate models enhances forecasting accuracy in terms of the magnitude of error, but the improvement is insufficient to produce a numerically smaller and statistically different RMSE compared to the random walk.

In Figure 4 we report the RMSE and alternative measures of forecasting accuracy for the random walk, the static version of the Frenkel-Bilson model and the TVP version of the same model. The TVP version is estimated by using the structural time series approach of Harvey (1989) and Doornik et al. (2006) whereby the final state vector is estimated by maximum likelihood and the Kalman filter. Looking at the root mean square error, we can see that TVP estimation boosts the forecasting power of the model, but the improvement is insufficient to outperform the random walk in a statistical sense.

However, the TVP model outperforms the random walk in all cases in terms of the ARMSE. This improvement is due to the fact that this particular TVP procedure introduces dynamics (Moosa and Burns, 2014a). We will come back to this point under proposition 11.

In terms of profitability, the TVP model outperforms the random walk consistently. And, needless to say, the TVP model outperforms the random walk in terms of proximity to a perfect forecast.

Thus, the use of TVP estimation does not resolve the Meese-Rogoff puzzle in the sense of producing a significantly lower RMSE than that of the random walk. But, just like in the case of the basic static model, the TVP model outperforms the random walk in terms of other measures of forecasting accuracy.

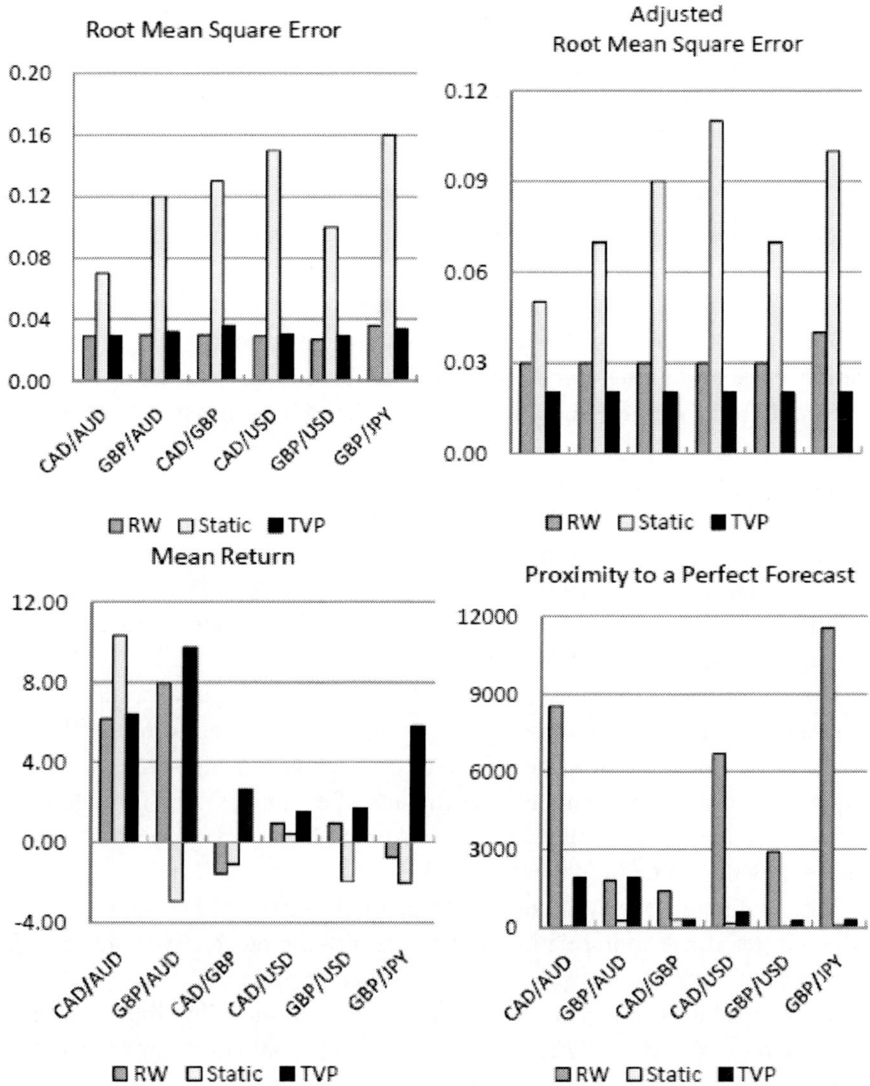

Figure 4. Measures of Forecasting Accuracy—TVP Frenkel-Bilson Model.

Proposition 8: Model Misspecification

The Meese-Rogoff puzzle cannot be explained by re-specifying conventional exchange rate models one way or another. Model specification refers to the process of converting a theory into an empirically testable representation, including the functional form of the model and the selection of explanatory variables. If an estimated model is misspecified, it will be biased and inconsistent—consequently, it performs poorly in a forecasting exercise (Lee and Lee., 1999). The literature suggests that the failure of conventional exchange rate models to outperform the random walk can be attributed to model misspecification. Engel (1999) argues that one of the most obvious problems of using the monetary model to forecast exchange rates is that the foundations of this model are unrealistic, which makes it misspecified.

Model misspecification may take a variety of forms. Meese and Rogoff (1983) suggest four possible types of misspecification: UIP, proxies for inflationary expectations, goods market specification and the money demand function. Others suggest that the monetary model is misspecified, simply because it is a stock rather than a flow model (Harvey, 2006). In addition, possible misspecifications include failure to distinguish between the prices of traded and non-traded goods (Balassa, 1964; Samuelson, 1964) and the imposition of the proportionality and symmetry restrictions (Neely and Sarno, 2002; Tawadros, 2001). Faust et al. (2003) argue that the monetary and portfolio balance models are "surely mis-specified in certain ways", referring to a combination of these forms of misspecification.

The empirical evidence suggests that monetary models suffer from specification errors, in the sense that important variables are omitted. Brooks et al. (2001), for example, find evidence indicating that the current account and portfolio flows are the main determinants of exchange rates. This suggests that the Frenkel-Bilson and Dornbusch-Frankel models are misspecified because they do not include these variables.

This argument is consistent with that of Anaraki (2007) who considers model misspecification in relation to the asset pricing mechanism and includes stock market returns in the monetary model. He argues that "traditional fundamental models have been mis-specified in the sense that they ignore the capital flows embedded in net foreign assets" and that equity portfolio flows can play a dominant role in capital flows and hence exchange rate movements. Lane and Milesi-Ferretti (2004) also find a strong, positive, long-run relation between international payments and the exchange rate.

An alternative approach to modelling exchange rate movements, proposed by Balassa (1964) and Samuelson (1964), distinguishes between the prices of traded and non-traded goods. In attempting to model exchange rate movements according to the price of traded and non-traded goods, Engel (1999) and Betts and Kehoe (2008) suggest that the producer price index (PPI) is more representative of the price of traded goods than the consumer price index (CPI). Betts and Kehoe (2001) examine the bilateral exchange rates and relative prices for 1225 currency pairs from 1980 to 2005 and find positive correlation between the two variables. In contrast, Groen and Lombardelli (2004) use a cointegrated VAR model and find no evidence indicating that movements in the exchange rate are determined by the relative price of traded and non-traded goods.

Another source of potential misspecification is the imposition of proportionality and symmetry restrictions on the monetary model. The symmetry restriction means that the value of the coefficients on the domestic variables and the corresponding foreign variables are equal, such that the model is specified in terms of relative variables (for example, the relative money supply, as opposed to the domestic money supply and foreign money supply as two separate variables). The symmetry restriction implies that elasticities are equal across the two countries.

Proportionality, on the other hand, is the condition that the coefficient on the relative money supply is equal to one. Neely and Sarno (2002) argue that "the failure of the [monetary] model may well be due to the failure of the symmetry and proportionality restrictions" and that these restrictions represent a "rather a strong assumption". Lane (1991) expresses a similar view.

The empirical evidence supports the proposition that exchange rate models are misspecified because they embed the assumptions of symmetry and proportionality (Cerrato and Sarantis, 2008). Cheung and Lai (1993) show the conventional symmetry and proportionality assumptions of exchange rate models are too restrictive. By relaxing the proportionality and symmetry restrictions, MacDonald and Taylor (1994) report that they manage to outperform the random walk.

However, the perceived improvement in the forecasting power of their model is due primarily to the use of dynamics, not the relaxation of the assumption of symmetry and proportionality. A restricted dynamic model produces better forecasts (in terms of the RMSE) than an unrestricted static model. This point will be examined under proposition 11.

The results supporting proposition 8 are presented in Figures 5, 6 and 7. In Figure 5, we report measures of forecasting accuracy for the random walk, the static version of the Frenkel-Bilson model and the Post-Keynesian (PK) model, which is a flow model that incorporates some dynamics (Harvey, 2006; Moosa, 2008). Again we find that the PK model introduces some improvement but fails to beat the random walk in terms of the RMSE.

However, the PK model generally outperforms the random walk in terms of the ARMSE, profitability and proximity to a perfect forecast.

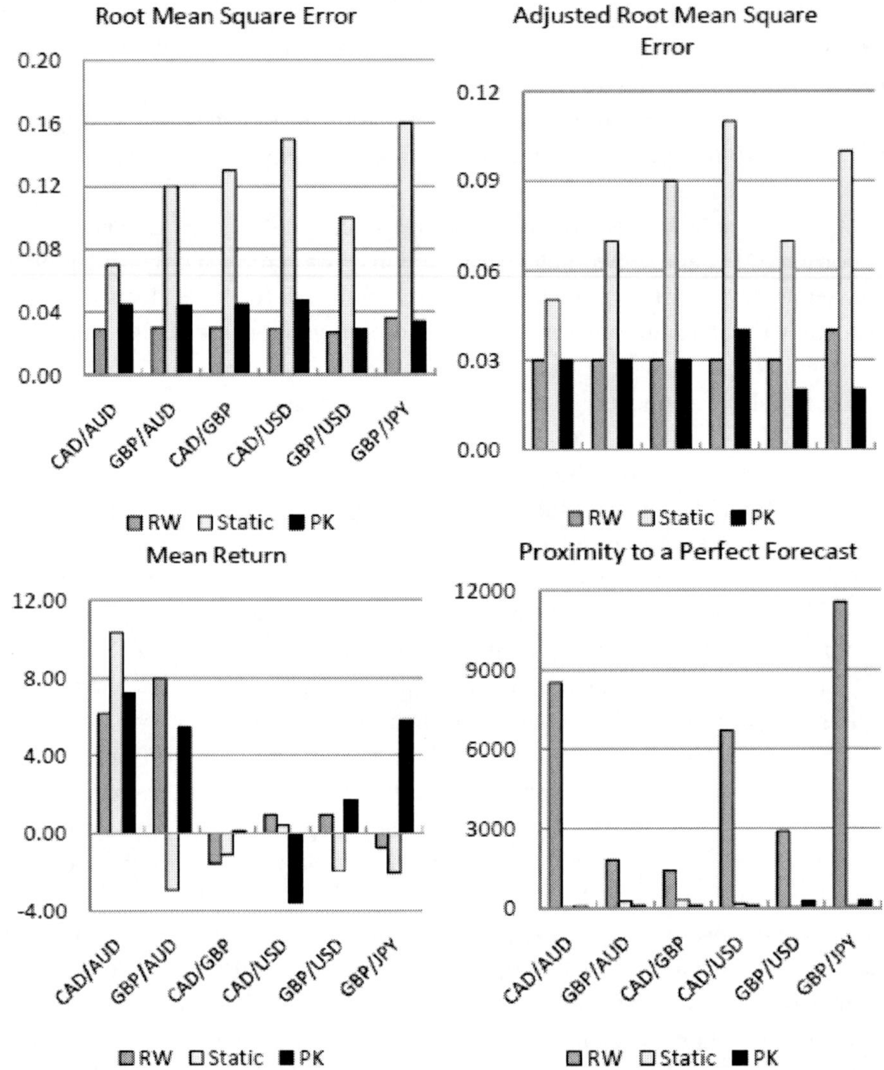

Figure 5. Measures of Forecasting Accuracy—Post-Keynesian Model.

In Figure 6 we report the same results for a version of the Frenkel-Bilson model that distinguishes between the prices of traded and non-traded goods (relative prices) but only for the CAD/USD (due to the unavailability of data on both the CPI and PPI for other countries). The model fails to outperform the random walk in terms of the RMSE and ARMSE but does much better in terms of profitability and proximity to a perfect forecast.

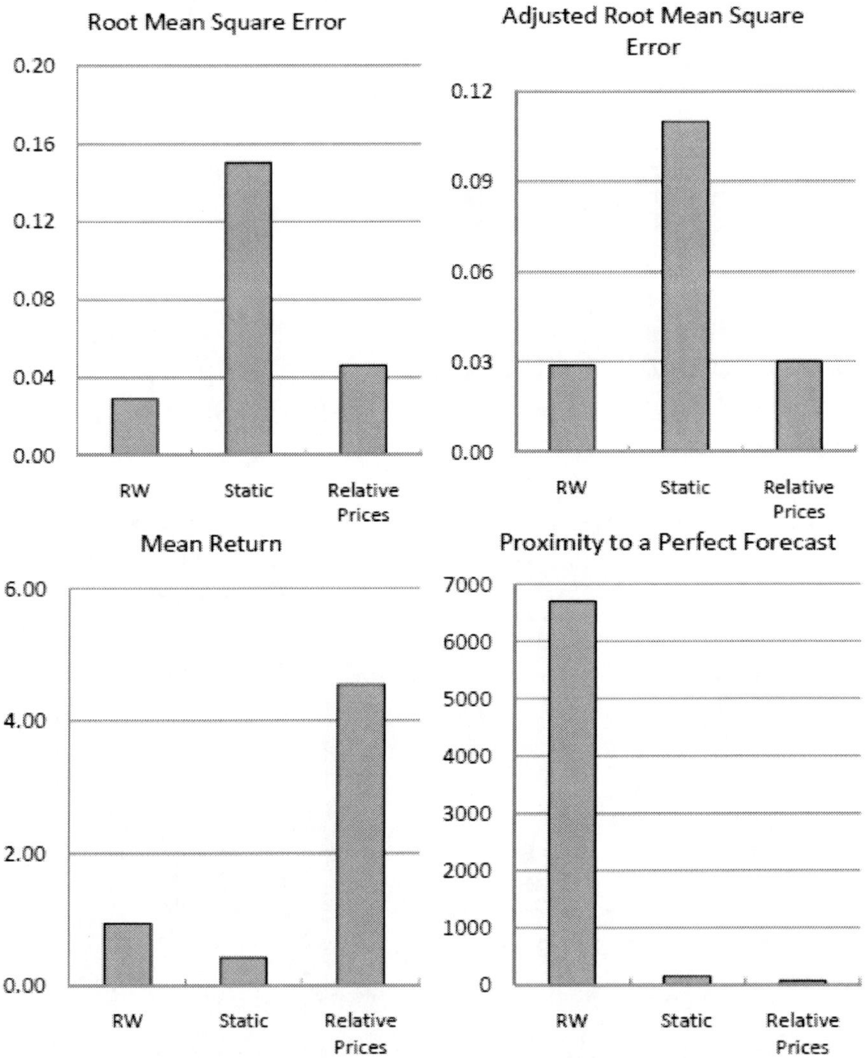

Figure 6. Measures of Forecasting Accuracy—Frenkel-Bilson Model With Relative Prices for CAD/USD.

In Figure 7, we report the same measures of forecasting accuracy for a model in which the proportionality and symmetry restrictions are relaxed.

It tells exactly the same story–the random walk cannot be outperformed in terms of magnitude-only measures of forecasting accuracy, but it can be outperformed by alternative metrics.

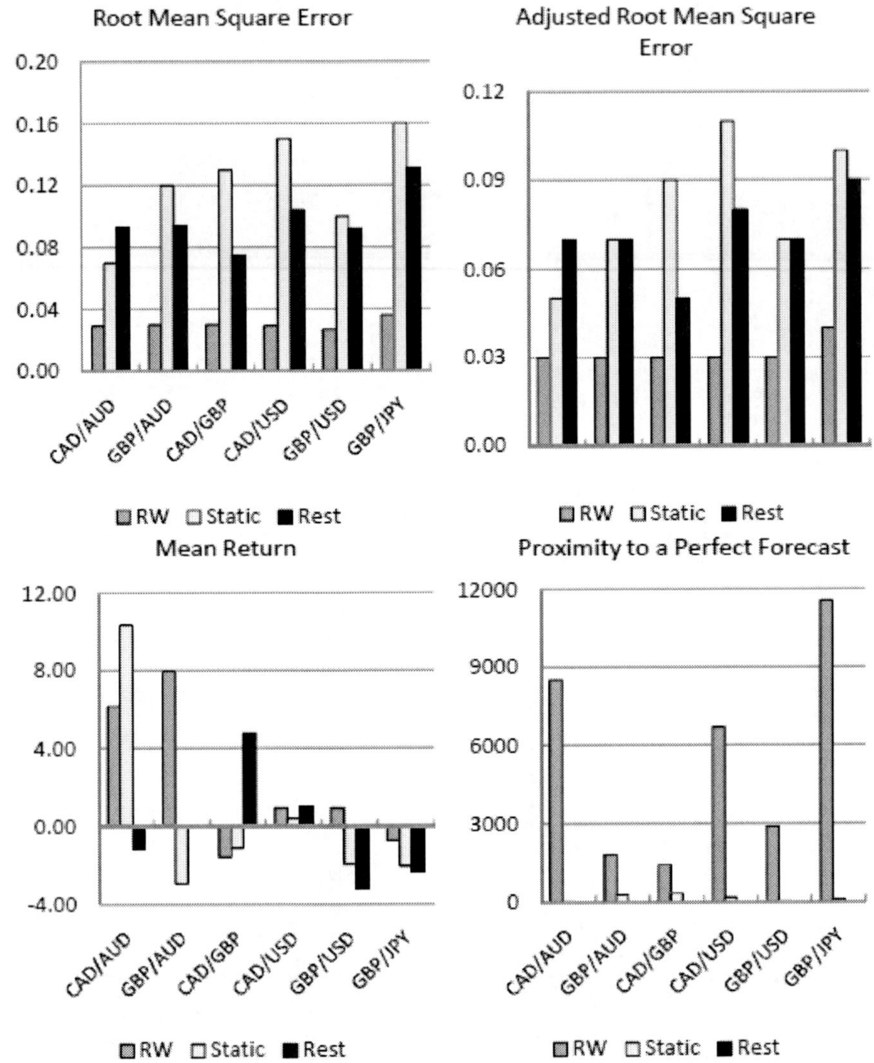

Figure 7. Measures of Forecasting Accuracy—Frenkel-Bilson Model Without Proportionality and Symmetry Restrictions.

PROPOSITION 9: INTRODUCING NON-LINEARITIES

The Meese-Rogoff puzzle cannot be resolved by using non-linear models. Meese and Rogoff (1983) suggest that inability to outperform the random walk may result from the use of exchange rate models that are linear in parameters when the exchange rate is a non-linear function of macroeconomic variables. It is well documented that many functional relations in finance are intrinsically non-linear (see, for example, Brooks, 2005). Taylor et al. (2001) point out that "the idea that there may be non-linearities in real exchange rate adjustment dates at least from Heckscher (1916)". If a non-linear relation exists between the exchange rate and macroeconomic variables, any attempt to fit a linear model to the data and generate forecasts with a smaller magnitude of error compared to the random walk will invariably fail. This sounds logical but it does not necessarily mean that any attempt to fit a non-linear model to the data and generate forecasts with a smaller magnitude of error compared to the random walk will invariably succeed. As we are going to find out, any such attempt will invariably fail.

Non-linearities can be accounted for in several ways, including the exponential smoothing transition autoregressive (ESTAR) technique (Kilian and Taylor, 2003; Brooks, 2005), introducing non-linear parameters, non-linear error correction models (Moosa, 1994), asymmetric moving average models (Elwood, 1998), floor/ceiling models (Pesaran and Potter, 1997) and Markov switching models (Hamilton, 1989). Taylor et al. (2001) suggest that ESTAR models are predominant in the (exchange rate) literature for two reasons: (i) they have the attractive property of allowing for "smooth transition between regimes and symmetric adjustment of the real exchange rate for deviations above and below the equilibrium level"; and (ii) they are relatively simplistic. Markov-switching models are popular because they capture the exchange rate adjustment process through a transition probability that is a function of the lagged deviation of the exchange rate from its equilibrium level. Many studies that use non-linear models of exchange rates focus on identifying whether or not a non-linear relation exists, as opposed to determining whether or not incorporating non-linearities enhances forecasting performance to the extent of outperforming the random walk.

For example, Taylor et al. (2001) fit a non-linear mean reverting (ESTAR) model to the dollar exchange rates in the post-Bretton Woods era (1973 to 1996) and report evidence of non-linear mean reversion.

The model implies stronger mean reversion the further away the exchange rate is from the equilibrium level. Taylor and Peel (2000) use an ESTAR model and conclude that exchange rates are almost unpredictable when macroeconomic variables are close to equilibrium values, but when they deviate from equilibrium by a large amount, the predictive power of the model improves because of strong reversion towards equilibrium.

Burns and Moosa (2014) demonstrate that the forecasting power of the conventional Frenkel-Bilson monetary model can be enhanced by specifying it as a non-linear error correction model with a polynomial in the error correction term. While the improvement in forecasting power relative to the static version is insufficient for the non-linear model to outperform the random walk in terms of the root mean square error, the model outperforms the random walk in terms of direction accuracy and profitability. More importantly, it is shown that the source of improvement in the forecasting accuracy of the model relative to the static version is the introduction of dynamics rather than non-linearities.

In Figure 8 we report measures of forecasting accuracy for the random walk, static model and a non-linear error correction model that contains a polynomial of order 3 in the error correction term. The results are reported only for the two exchange rates where we obtain significant non-linear error correction terms. The non-linear model cannot outperform the random walk in terms of the RMSE but it can in terms of the ARMSE, profitability and proximity to a perfect forecast. As in the TVP case, improvement over the static model is due to the introduction of dynamics rather than non-linearities.

Proposition 10: Simultaneous Equation Models

The Meese-Rogoff puzzle cannot be resolved by using simultaneous equation models. Simultaneous equation bias arises due to endogeneity and is considered to be one of the most significant econometric problems the Meese and Rogoff (1983) study suffers from (Neely and Sarno, 2002).

The potential for endogeneity to exist between exchange rates and the explanatory variables is well documented (Thoma, 2008; Engel and West, 2005; Molodsova and Papell, 2008). Endogeneity would occur, for example, when central banks take exchange rates into account when they set the cash rate. Engel et al. (2007) also highlight the role of monetary policy endogeneity in explaining nominal and real exchange rate behaviour.

Likewise, Engel and West (2005) and Molodsova and Papell (2008) draw attention to the potential for monetary policy feedback as a form of endogeneity. Neely and Sarno (2002) argue that all of the explanatory variables of the monetary model are endogenous, which means that the estimated coefficients are likely to suffer from simultaneous equation bias.

According to Gandolfo et al. (1990), “the exchange rate is just one of the endogenous variables of an economy-wide model”.

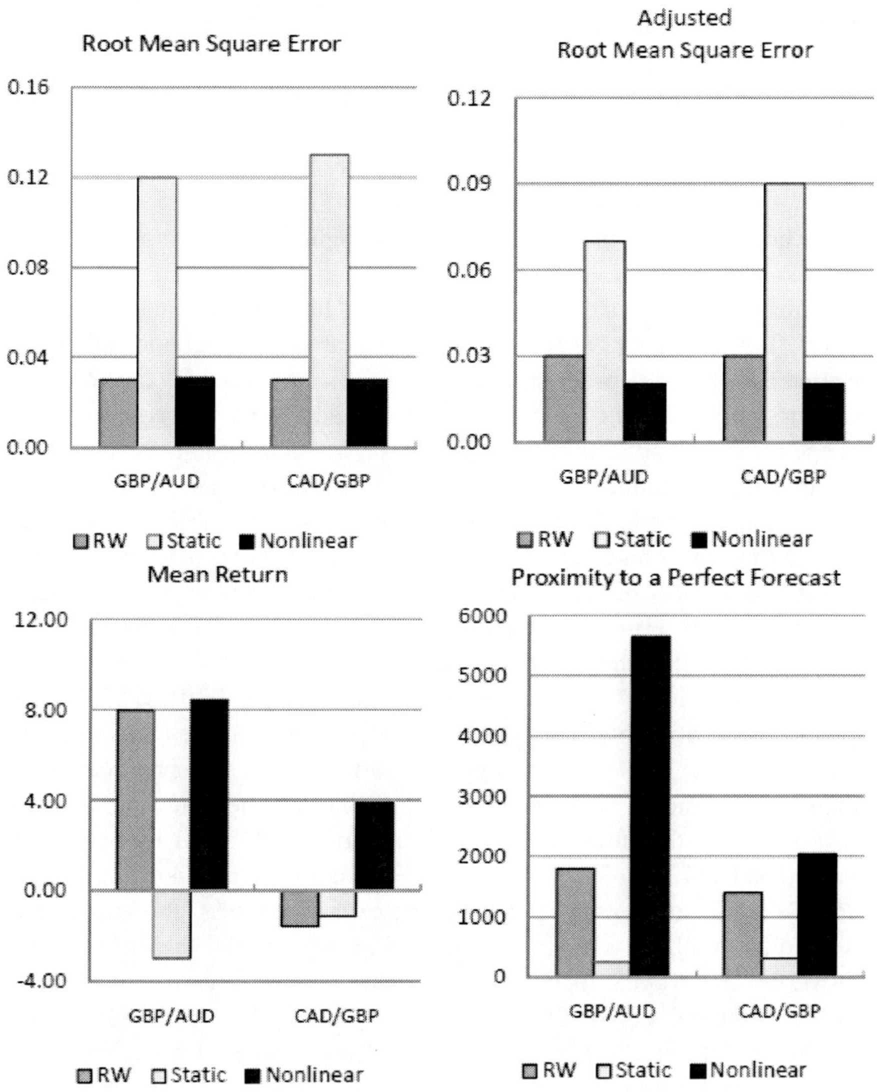

Figure 8. Measures of Forecasting Accuracy—Frenkel-Bilson Non-linear Error Correction Model for GBP/AUD and CAD/GBP.

Isard (1987) suggests that the Meese-Rogoff puzzle is attributed to the use of single-equation semi-reduced form models. He argues that "models that simultaneously take account of a complete system of macroeconomic relationships will be able to improve on the single-equation, semi-reduced form models in capturing the associations between exchange rates, interest differentials, and other variables". Likewise, Gandolfo et al. (1990) contend that "only by moving away from these single-equation, semi-reduced form models towards suitable economy-wide macroeconometric models can one hope to beat the random walk".

The use of the word "hope" here is highly appropriate if "beating the random walk" is determined in terms of the RMSE. If this is the case we can certainly hope, but we will invariably be disappointed.

Economists use various techniques to account for simultaneous equation bias with varying degrees of success (or failure). In their original study, Meese and Rogoff used Fair's (1970) instrumental variables technique to estimate an unrestricted VAR in order to correct for simultaneous equation bias. Specifying exchange rate models as a VAR addresses the possible linear interdependencies among multiple time series, as each variable is represented by an equation explaining its evolution, based (linearly) on its own lags as well as the contemporaneous and lagged values of all other variables in the model. Similarly, Berkowitz and Giorgianni (2001) use an unrestricted VAR and find very little evidence of predictability. In contrast, Kilian (1999) uses a constrained vector error correction model to generate forecasts using the technique of feasible generalised least squares.

Some evidence has emerged to suggest that using a VAR to account for simultaneous equation bias can boost forecasting performance (Carriero et al., 2009). Brannstrom (1995), for example, reports that a VAR specification can outperform the random walk in the short run but not the long run. Gandolfo et al. (1990) use the three monetary models originally used by Meese and Rogoff (1983) and a Mark V version of the continuous time macroeconometric model of the Italian economy to predict the exchange rate of the lira *vis-à-vis* the US dollar. Without testing the statistical significance of the differences in the RMSEs and MAEs, they conclude that "our continuous time macro-econometric model of the Italian economy outperforms both the existing structural models and the random walk". They argue that exchange rate movements cannot be explained or accurately forecast using single-equation semi-reduced form models because these models only provide "a partial view of exchange-rate determination". While it is true that a comprehensive multi-equation model is more representative of the working of the economy, the use of a multi-equation model is not necessarily conducive to the production of more accurate forecasts. Again, "numerically smaller" does not count.

Although some studies conclude that the random walk can be outperformed by a VAR model, these findings are questionable on two grounds. First, no test is performed to find out if the difference in the RMSEs of the model and random walk is statistically significant. Second, a VAR specification introduces a lagged dependent variable, which is a random walk component. This is why the empirical evidence indicates that a VAR specification produces superior forecasting performance in terms of the numerical magnitude of error (Brannstrom, 1995). If at all, it is dynamics (not the removal of simultaneous equation bias) that beats the random walk in terms of the magnitude of the error (if that is possible at all).

PROPOSITION 11: THE USE OF DYNAMIC SPECIFICATIONS

The specification of the monetary models in a static rather than a dynamic form is one possible source of model misspecification. Some economists have attempted to address this problem by specifying the monetary model in a dynamic form, such as first difference, error correction and distributed lags (see, for example, Cheung et al., 2005). MacDonald and Taylor (1993) use a dynamic error correction model and conclude (without testing the statistical significance of the difference) that the model forecasts are superior to those of the random walk. Not surprisingly, similar results are obtained by MacDonald and Taylor (1994) who use an error correction specification of the monetary model and conclude that "the estimated model clearly outperforms the random walk (with and without drift) across a range of forecasting horizons". Again, MacDonald and Taylor (1994) fail to test for the significance of the difference in the magnitude of forecasting errors.

We do not claim that dynamic specifications are an inaccurate representation of the actual behaviour of variables, but rather that they are not suitable for a forecasting exercise that is intended to find out if the random walk can be beaten. The use of dynamics implicitly and effectively introduces a lagged dependent variable, which makes the underlying model some sort of an "augmented" random walk (Moosa and Burns, 2014b).

The random walk component, represented by the lagged dependent variable, invariably dominates the effect of the explanatory variables. The coefficient on the lagged dependent variable tends to be close to one, which causes two problems (Kling, 2011).

First, it makes the models relatively unstable and results in a loss of explanatory power. Kling (2011) argues that while the most "accurate" (in terms of the RMSE) forecasting models include lagged dependent variables, "the resulting equations often have structural properties that are not desired by the model builders".

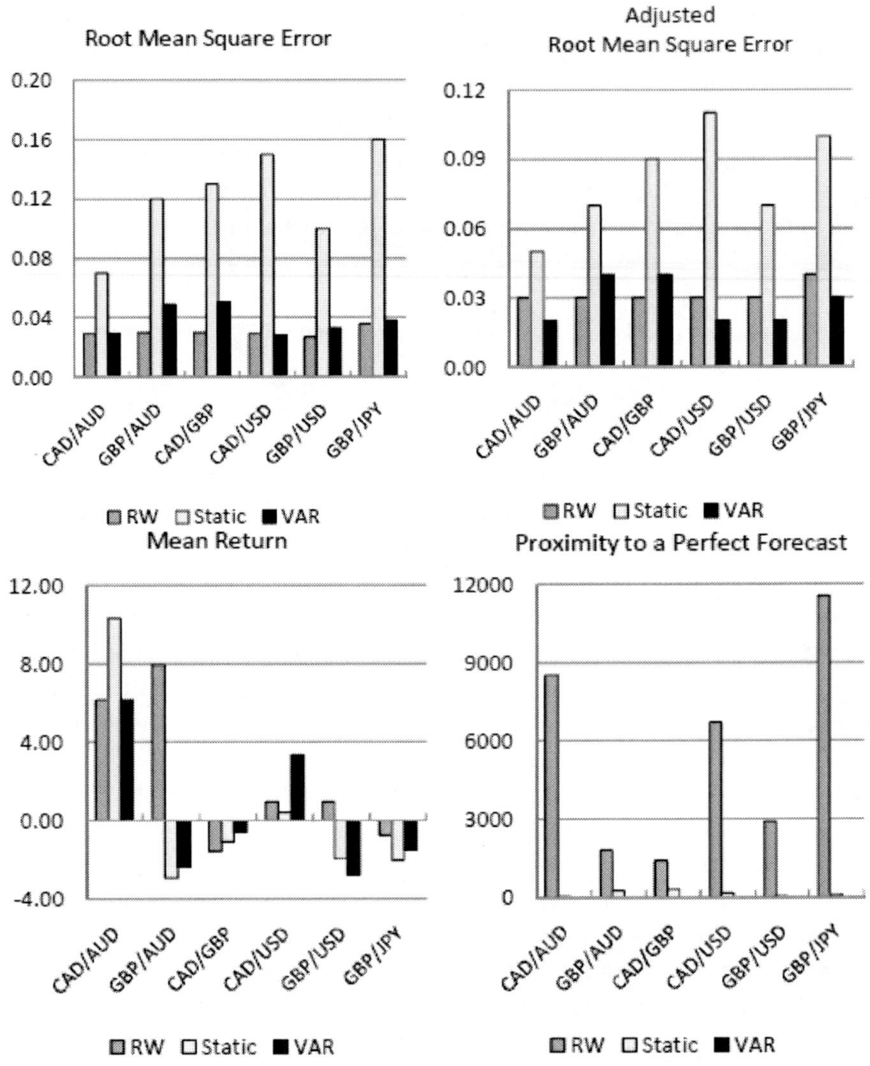

Figure 9. Measures of Forecasting Accuracy—Frenkel-Bilson VAR Model.

Second, and more importantly, the dominance of the lagged dependent variable makes the forecasts look exactly like those generated by a random walk.

Moosa and Burns (2014b) show that dynamics of any form produces a lagged dependent variable, which makes the model behave like the random walk and make the forecasts generated by the model resemble the forecasts generated by the random walk.

This point is illustrated in Figure 10, which shows scatter diagrams of the forecasts of the model and those of the random walk. We can readily observe that correlation between forecasts is weaker in the cases of the basic static model and the static model without the proportionality and symmetry restrictions. Correlation is stronger in the case of the Post-Keynesian model and almost perfect for the non-linear error correction model, the TVP model and the VAR, all of which involve dynamics.

Therefore, claiming to outperform the random walk with a dynamic model (which does not happen if appropriate testing of significance is conducted) is like claiming to outperform the random walk with a random walk. Not even a dynamic model specification can produce significantly a lower RMSE than the random walk.

PROPOSITION 12: SAMPLING ERRORS

The Meese-Rogoff puzzle cannot be resolved by manipulating the sample size or the split between the estimation and forecasting periods. Meese and Rogoff (1983), and several other economists, suggest that sampling errors may explain the inability of exchange rate models to outperform the random walk in forecasting exchange rates movements.

Given the numerous unsuccessful attempts to overturn the Meese-Rogoff findings using different sample periods, exchange rates and sample breaks, one tends to think that sampling errors cannot explain the Meese-Rogoff puzzle. Indeed, there is no standard for judging and identifying sampling errors to decide which sample period is right and which is wrong.

Any choice is bound to be arbitrary or subjective. But some economists believe that sampling errors may resolve the Meese-Rogoff puzzle and that the forecasting power of exchange rate models is sensitive to sample selection (for example, Faust et al., 2003; Cheung et al., 2005).

Some studies suggest that the length of the estimation window is important because using additional historical observations enhances forecasting performance (Kirikos, 2000). The literature also points towards the selection of the forecasting window as influencing forecasting performance, because a model that performs well for one currency at one point in time may not work well for that currency over time (Cheung et al., 2005). The evidence also indicates that changes in the split of the sample between the forecasting and estimation periods is consequential for forecasting performance (Kirikos, 2000; Cheung et al., 2005).

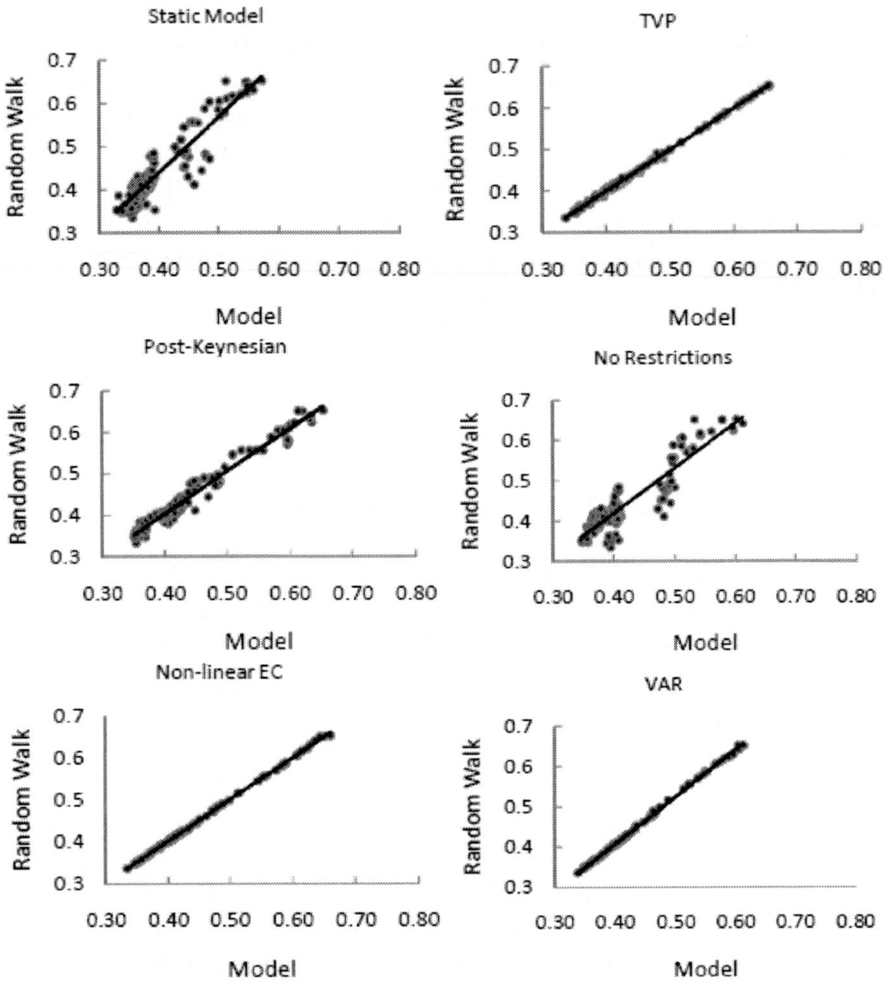

Figure 10. Correlation of Model Forecasts with the Random Walk.

Other studies suggest that a small sample size has an adverse effect on the ability of exchange rate models to outperform the random walk in terms of the magnitude of error (Anaraki, 2007; Kirikos, 2000; Cheung et al., 2005; Engel and West, 2005).

These are valid arguments, but it is unlikely that any potential improvement would overturn the Meese-Rogoff results in a narrow sense.

The findings produced by Moosa and Burns (2013a) suggest that sample size may impact the forecasting accuracy of exchange rate models in terms of profitability.

They show that the random walk consistently outperforms the models in terms of profitability (measured by mean returns and proportion of positive returns). The consistent superiority of the model forecasts in terms of profitability, as reported by Moosa and Burns (2013a), may be attributable to shorter sample periods that are characterised by mean returns with low standard deviations. Therefore, it can be inferred that sample size impacts the performance of exchange rate models relative to the random walk when forecasting accuracy is assessed by alternative measures such as profitability.

The results presented so far are based on the use of approximately 17 years of monthly data as the estimation window and a forecasting window of approximately 10 years. In this exercise we reduce the estimation period to July 1989-June 2001 (12 years) and retain the original forecasting period (10 years). In Figure 11 we report measures of forecasting accuracy for the basic Frenkel-Bilson model using the original sample (static) and the modified sample (sample). Nothing much happens as a result of this change. The random walk still outperforms the model in terms of the RMSE but not in terms of other measures of forecasting accuracy. Other possible changes make no difference whatsoever (see, for example, Moosa and Burns, 2014c).

Proportion 13: Inflationary Expectations

It is not possible to resolve the Meese-Rogoff puzzle by trying different proxies for inflationary expectations. Expectations play an important role in the monetary models of exchange rates because the long-run expected inflation rate is an explanatory variable in both the Dornbusch-Frankel and Hooper-Morton models. It has been suggested that improper modelling of inflationary expectations may explain the Meese-Rogoff puzzle, but inflationary expectations are unobservable, which makes the measurement of this variable difficult and even subjective. In the words of Meese and Rogoff (1983) modelling or measuring expectations (particularly inflationary expectations) "presents many problems".

Monetary models of exchange rates are potentially very sensitive to the measure selected to proxy this variable, which means that improper modelling may explain the poor performance of these models in terms of the RMSE. Meese and Rogoff (1983) suggest three proxies for inflationary expectations: the actual preceding 12-month inflation rate, the value estimated from an inflation rate autoregression, and the long-term interest rate differential (which they elect to use).

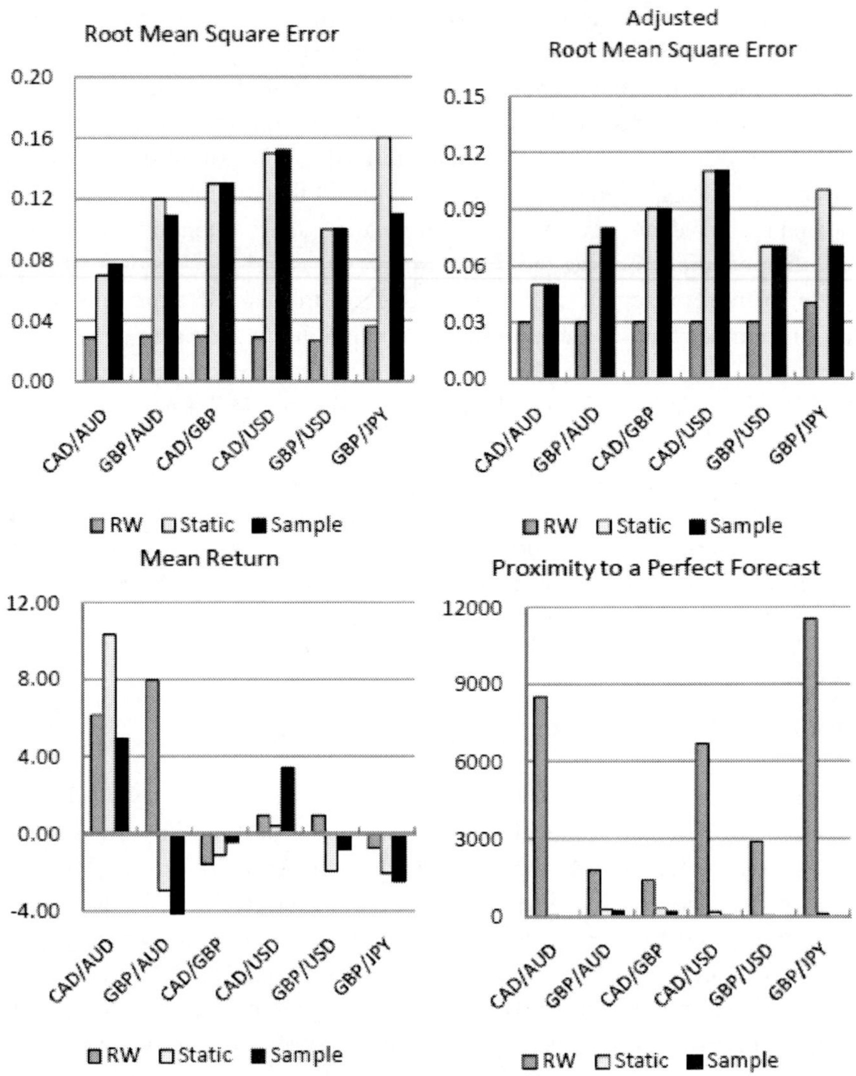

Figure 11. Measures of Forecasting Accuracy—Frenkel-Bilson Model With Modified Sample Period.

The question addressed in this section is whether or not using alternative measures of inflationary expectations enhances the forecasting power of the monetary model to the extent that it outperforms the random walk in terms of the RMSE. The point that seems to be overlooked is that the measures of expected inflation used by Meese and Rogoff and others are arbitrary—they are very unlikely to be a reflection of the true market expectation that can be derived from a survey.

The appropriateness of competing expectation formation mechanisms has been widely debated in the literature. Inflationary expectations can be represented by extrapolative, rational and adaptive expectations. Extrapolative expectations imply positive dependence in period-to-period changes in the underlying variable (inflation, in this case). This means that a rise in inflation is expected to be followed by another rise, and vice versa. The empirical evidence supports the existence of extrapolative expectations in the foreign exchange market (Moosa and Shamsuddin, 2004). Under adaptive expectations, on the other hand, agents (market participants) form their expectations of the future on the basis of what happened in the past. According to this mechanism, if expectations are wrong, future expectations are revised according to the realised expectation error. In contrast, Engel et al. (2007) measure inflationary expectations by using surveys of professional forecasters. Moosa and Shamsuddin (2004) put forward three arguments against using survey data: (i) data reliability, (ii) disconnectedness between inflationary expectations and actual movements, and (iii) biasness in survey results. Notwithstanding these problems, surveys provide a true reflection of expectations that cannot be provided by econometric methods.

The empirical evidence suggests that expectation formation is time-varying. Several studies reveal a reversal in the direction of expectations over long periods of time. MacDonald (2000) describes this phenomenon as a "twist" in expectation formation. Based on a survey of the literature, he concludes that forecasting at horizons longer than three months exhibits clear evidence indicating that expectations are stabilising. This means that long-run expectations typically indicate movement towards equilibrium, whereas short-run expectations point to movement away from equilibrium. Therefore, the choice between proxy measures of inflationary expectations should also take into account the forecasting horizon.

In Figure 12 we report measures of forecasting accuracy for the Dornbusch-Frankel model when it is estimated with four different expectation formation mechanisms: static, weighted average, moving average and geometrically declining distributed lags (GDL). We do not observe any change in forecasting accuracy across various expectation formation mechanisms. More importantly, it makes no difference to the findings—the model cannot outperform the random walk in terms of the RMSE. Playing with the expectation formation mechanism is not the way to resolve the Meese-Rogoff puzzle.

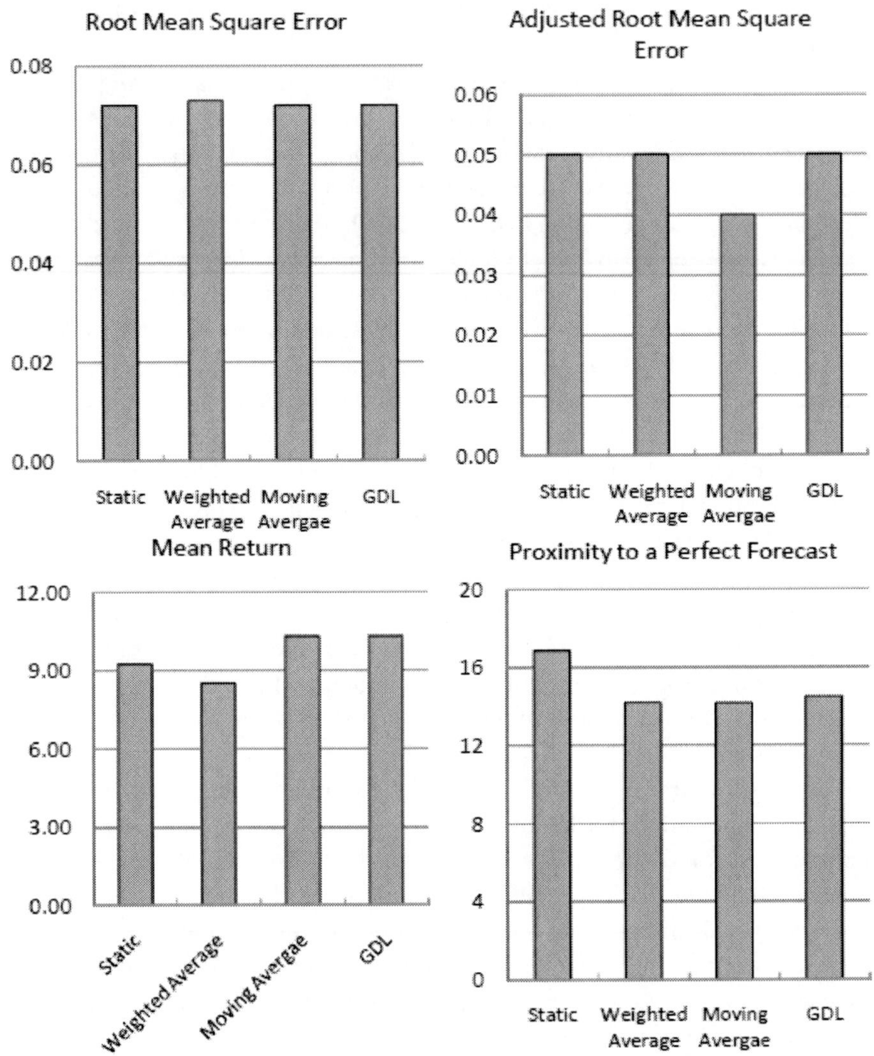

Figure 12. Measures of Forecasting Accuracy—Dornbusch-Frankel Model With Various Inflationary Expectations.

Conclusion

In 1983 the Meese-Rogoff puzzle was born when Richard Meese and Kenneth Rogoff published results showing that exchange rate models cannot outperform the random walk in out-of-sample forecasting.

Following the arguments and the evidence presented in this chapter we can conclude that the puzzle is not really a puzzle and that we should not expect anything other than the fact that no model can outperform the random walk in out-of-sample (and in-sample) forecasting. We have demonstrated that the reasons suggested by Meese and Rogoff for the inability of the models to outperform the random walk are not valid in the sense that none of the implied modifications makes any change to the conclusions reached. We have also shown that attempting to outperform the random walk with a dynamic model is tantamount to attempting to beat the random walk with a random walk. Most importantly, however, it is easy to outperform the random walk by using measures of forecasting accuracy other than those that depend only on the magnitude of the forecasting error such as the RMSE. The Meese-Rogoff puzzle is not a puzzle in any shape or form.

References

Abhyankar, A., Sarno, L. and Valente, G. (2005) Exchange Rates and Fundamentals: Evidence on the Economic Value of Predictability, *Journal of International Economics*, 66, 325-348.

Anaraki, N. (2007) Meese and Rogoff's Puzzle Revisited, *International Review of Business Research Papers,* 3, 278-304.

Ashley, R., Granger, C. and Schmalensee, R. (1980) Advertising and Aggregate Consumption: An Analysis of Causality, *Econometrica,* 48, 1149-67.

Bacchetta, P. and van Wincoop, E. (2006) Can Information Heterogeneity Explain the Exchange Rate Determination Puzzle?, *American Economic Review*, 96, 552-576.

Balassa, B. (1964) The Purchasing Power Parity Doctrine: A Reappraisal, *Journal of Political Economy*, 72, 584-96.

Berkowitz, J. and Giorgianni, L. (2001) Long Horizon Exchange Rate Predictability, *Review of Economics and Statistics,* 83, 81-91.

Betts, C. and Kehoe, T. (2001) *Tradability of Goods and Real Exchange Rate Fluctuations,* University of Minnesota, Department of Economics. Mimeographed.

Betts, C. and Kehoe, T. (2008) Real Exchange Rate Movements and the Relative Price of Non-traded Goods, *NBER Working Paper*, 14437.

Brannstrom, T. (1995) *Bias Approximation and Reduction in Vector Autoregressive Models*, Dissertation for the Doctor's Degree in

Philosophy, Department of Economic Statistics, Stockholm School of Economics.

Brooks, C. (2005) *Introductory Econometrics for Finance*, Cambridge: University Press.

Brooks, R., Kumar, E. and Slok, T. (2001) Exchange Rate and Capital Flows, *IMF Working Paper,* 01/190.

Burns, K. and Moosa, I. A. (2014) Enhancing the Forecasting Power of Exchange Rate Models by Introducing Nonlinearities: Does it Work?, *Working Paper*.

Carriero, A., Kapetanios, G. and Marcellino, M. (2009) Forecasting Exchange Rates with a Large Bayesian VAR, *International Journal of Forecasting*, 25, 400-417.

Cerrato, M. and Sarantis, N. (2008) Symmetry, Proportionality and the Purchasing Power Parity: Evidence From Panel Cointegration Tests, *International Review of Economics and Finance*, 17, 56-65.

Cheung, Y., Chinn, M. and Pascual, A. (2005) Empirical Exchange Rate Models of the Nineties: Are They Fit to Survive?, *Journal of International Money and Finance*, 24, 1150-1175.

Cheung, Y. and Lai, K. (1993), Long-Run Purchasing Power Parity During the Recent Float, *Journal of International Economics*, 34, 181-192.

Christoffersen, P. and Diebold, F. (1998) Cointegration and Long-Horizon Forecasting, *Journal of Business and Economic Statistics*, 16, 450-58.

Corte, P., Lucio, S. and Tsiakas, I. (2009) An Economic Evaluation of Empirical Exchange Rate Models, *Review Financial Studies,* 22, 3491-3530.

Diebold, F. and Mariano, R. (1995) Comparing Predictive Accuracy, *Journal of Business and Economic Statistics*, 13, 253-263.

Doornik, J. (2006) *Object-Oriented Matrix Programming using Ox*, 5th edition, London: Timberlake Consultants Press.

Elwood, S. (1998) Is the Persistence of Shocks to Output Asymmetric?, *Journal of Monetary Economics,* 41, 411-26.

Engel, C. (1994) Can the Markov Switching Model Forecast Exchange Rates? *Journal of International Economics*, 36, 151-165.

Engel, C. (1999) Accounting for US Real Exchange Rate Changes, *Journal of Political Economy,* 107, 507-38.

Engel, C. and Hamilton, J. (1990) Long Swings in the Dollar: Are They in the Data and Do Markets Know it?, *American Economic Review*, 80, 689-713.

Engel, C., Mark, N. and West, K. (2007) Exchange Rate Models are Not as Bad as You Think, *NBER Macroeconomics Annual*, 22, 381-441.

Engel, C. and West, K. (2005) Exchange Rates and Fundamentals, *Journal of Political Economy*, 113, 485-517.

Evans, M. and Lyons, R. (2004) A New Micro Model of Exchange Rate Dynamics, *NBER Working Papers, No 10379.*

Evans, M. and Lyons, R. (2005) Meese-Rogoff Redux: Micro-Based Exchange Rate Forecasting, *American Economic Review*, 965, 405-414.

Fair, R. (1970) The Estimation of Simultaneous Equation Models with Lagged Endogenous Variables and First Order Serially Correlated Errors, *Econometrica*, 3, 507-516.

Fair, R. (2008) Estimating Exchange Rate Equations Using Estimated Expectations, *Yale University ICF Working Paper No. 07-18.*

Faust, J., Rogers, J. and Wright, J. (2003) Exchange Rate Forecasting: The Errors We've Really Made, *Journal of International Economics,* 60, 35-39.

Flood, R. and Rose, A. (2008) Why So Glum? The Meese-Rogoff Methodology Meets the Stock Market, *CEPR Discussion Papers*, 6714.

Frankel, J. and Rose, A. (1995) Empirical Research on Nominal Exchange Rates, *Handbook of International Economics*, 3, Amsterdam: Elsevier.

Frommel, M., MacDonald, R. and Menkhoff, L. (2005) Do Fundamentals Matter for the D-Mark/Euro-Dollar? A Regime Switching Approach, *Global Finance Journal*, 15, 321-335.

Gandolfo, G., Padoan, P. and Paladino, G. (1990) Structural Models vs. Random Walk: The Case of the Lira/$ Exchange Rate, *Eastern Economic Journal,* 16, 101-113.

Groen, J. (1999) Long Horizon Predictability of Exchange Rates: Is It For Real?, *Empirical Economics,* 24, 451-469.

Groen, J. and Lombardelli, C. (2004) Real Exchange Rates and the Relative Prices of Non-traded and Traded Goods: An Empirical Analysis, *Bank of England Working Paper,* No. 223.

Hamilton, J. (1989) A New Approach to the Economic Analysis of Nonstationary Time Series and the Business Cycle, *Econometrica,* 57, 357-84.

Harvey, A. (1989) *Forecasting, Structural Time Series Models and the Kalman Filter*, Cambridge: Cambridge University Press.

Harvey, J. (2006) Post Keynesian versus Neoclassical Explanations of Exchange Rate Movements: A Short Look at the Long Run, *Journal of Post Keynesian Economics*, 28, 161-179.

Heckscher, E. (1916) Vaxelkursens Grundval vid Pappersmyntfot, *Ekono-misk Tidskrift,* 18, 309-12.

Isard, P. (1987) Lessons from Empirical Models of Exchange Rates, *International Monetary Fund Staff Papers,* 34, 1-28.

Juntilla, J. and Korhonen, M. (2011) Nonlinearity and Time-variation in the Monetary Model of Exchange Rates, *Journal of Macroeconomics*, 33, 288-302.

Kilian, L. (1999) Exchange Rates and Monetary Fundamentals: What Do We Learn From Long-Horizon Regressions?, *Journal of Applied Econometrics,* 14, 491-510.

Kilian, L. and Taylor, M. (2003) Why is it so Difficult to Beat the Random Walk Forecast of Exchange Rates?, *Journal of International Economics*, 60, 85-107.

Kirikos, D. (2000) Forecasting Exchange Rates Out-of-sample: Random Walk vs. Markov Switching Regimes, *Applied Economics Letters*, 7, 133-136.

Kling, A. (2011) Macroeconomics: The Science of Hubris, *Critical Review*, 23, 123-133.

Lane, T. D. (1991) Empirical Models of Exchange-Rate Determination: Picking Up the Pieces, *Economia Internazionale*, 44, 210-227.

Lane, P. and Milesi-Ferretti, G. (2004) The Transfer Problem Revisited: Net Foreign Assets and Real Exchange Rates, *The Review of Economics and Statistics,* 86, 841-857.

Lee, C., John, C. and Lee, A. (1999) *Statistics for Business and Financial Economics*, 2nd edn., Singapore: World Scientific Publishing Company.

Leitch, G. and Tanner, J. (1991) Economic Forecast Evaluation: Profits versus the Conventional Error Measures, *American Economic Review*, 81, 580-590.

Li, M. (2011) An Evaluation of Exchange Rate Models by Carry Trade, *Journal of Economics and International Finance*, 3, 72-87.

MacDonald, R. (2000) Expectations Formation and Risk in Three Financial Markets: Surveying What the Surveys Say, *Journal of Economic Surveys,* 14, 68-100.

MacDonald, R. and Taylor, M. (1993) The Monetary Approach to the Exchange Rate: Rational Expectations, Long-Run Equilibrium and Forecasting, *IMF Staff Papers*, 40, 89-107.

MacDonald, R. and Taylor, M. (1994) The Monetary Model of the Exchange Rate: Long-Run Relationships, Short-Run Dynamics and How to Beat a Random Walk, *Journal of International Money and Finance,* 13, 276-290.

Meese, R. and Rogoff, K. (1983) Empirical Exchange Rate Models of the Seventies: Do They Fit Out-of-sample? *Journal of International Economics*, 14, 3-24.

Molodsova, T. and Papell, D. (2008) Out-of-sample Exchange Rate Predictability with Taylor Rule Fundamentals, *Journal of International Economics,* 77, 167-180.

Moosa, I. A. (1994) Testing Nonlinearities in Purchasing Power Parity, *Applied Economics Letters*, 1, 41-43.

Moosa, I. A. (2000) *Exchange Rate Forecasting: Techniques and Applications*, London: Macmillan.

Moosa, I. A. (2004a) What is Wrong with Market-Based Forecasting of Exchange Rates?, *International Journal of Business and Economics*, 3, 107-121.

Moosa, I. A. (2004b) Is Covered Interest Parity an Arbitrage or a Hedging Condition?, *Economia Internazionale*, 57, 189-194.

Moosa, I. A. (2006) On the Notion of Forecasting Accuracy as Applied to Financial Decision Rules Involving Exchange Rates, *Forecasting Letters*, 1, 5-9.

Moosa, I. A. (2008) Neoclassical Versus Post Keynesian Models of Exchange Rate Determination: A Comparison Based on Non-nested Model Selection Tests and Predictive Accuracy, *Journal of Post Keynesian Economics*, 30, 169-185.

Moosa, I. A. (2013) Why is it so Difficult to Outperform the Random Walk in Exchange Rate Forecasting, *Applied Economics,* 23, 3340-3346.

Moosa, I. A. and Burns, K. (2012) Can Exchange Rate Models Outperform the Random Walk? Magnitude, Direction and Profitability as Criteria, *Economia Internazionale*, 65, 473-490.

Moosa, I. A. and Burns, K. (2013a) A Reappraisal of the Meese-Rogoff Puzzle, *Applied Economics,* 46, 30-40.

Moosa, I. A. and Burns, K. (2013b) The Monetary Model of Exchange Rates is Better than the Random Walk in Out-Of-Sample Forecasting, *Applied Economics Letters,* 20, 1293-1297.

Moosa, I. A. and Burns, K. (2014a) The Unbeatable Random Walk in Exchange Rate Forecasting: Reality or Myth?, *Journal of Macroeconomics*, 40, 69-81.

Moosa, I. A. and Burns, K. (2014b) Error Correction Modelling and Dynamic Specifications as a Conduit to Outperforming the Random Walk in Exchange Rate Forecasting, *Applied Economics*, 46, 3107-3118.

Moosa, I. A. and Burns, K. (2014c) *Demystifying the Meese-Rogoff Puzzle*, London: Palgrave (forthcoming).

Moosa, I. A. and Shamsuddin, A. (2004) Expectation Formation Mechanisms, Profitability of Foreign Exchange Trading and Exchange Rate Volatility, *Applied Economics,* 36, 1599-1606.

Moosa, I. A. and Vaz, J. (2014) Why is it so Difficult to Outperform the Random Walk? An Application of the Meese-Rogoff Puzzle to Stock Prices, *Applied Economics* (forthcoming).

Neely, C. and Sarno, L. (2002) How Well Do Monetary Fundamentals Forecast Exchange Rates, *Review*, Federal Reserve Bank of St. Louis, September Issue, 51-74.

Pesaran, H. and Potter, S. (1997) A Floor and Ceiling Model of US Output, *Journal of Economic Dynamics and Controls,* 21, 661-96.

Rossi, B. (2006) Are Exchange Rates Really Random Walks? Some Evidence Robust to Parameter Instability, *Macroeconomic Dynamics,* 10, 20-38.

Samuelson, P. (1964) Theoretical Notes on Trade Problems, *Review of Economics and Statistics*, 46, 145-54.

Schinasi, G. and Swamy, P. (1989) The Out-of-Sample Forecasting Performance of Exchange Rate Models when Coefficients are Allowed to Change, *Journal of International Money and Finance*, 8, 375-390.

Tawadros, G. (2001) The Predictive Power of the Monetary Model of Exchange Rate Determination, *Applied Financial Economics*, 11, 279-286.

Taylor, M. and Peel, D. (2000) Non-linear Adjustment, Long-run Equilibrium and Exchange Rate Fundamentals, *Journal of International Money and Finance,* 19, 22-54.

Taylor, M., Peel, D. and Sarno, L. (2001) Nonlinear Mean-Reversion in Real Exchange Rates: Toward a Solution to the Purchasing Power Parity Puzzles, *International Economic Review*, 42, 1015-1042.

Thoma, M. (2008) FRB Dallas: Why Are Exchange Rates So Difficult to Predict?, *Economonitor,* July 22 2008.

West, K., Edison, H. and Cho, D. (1993) A Utility Based Comparison of Some Models of Exchange Rate Volatility, *Journal of International Economics*, 35, 23-45.

Wolff, C. (1987) Time-Varying Parameters and the Out-of-Sample Forecasting Performance of Structural Exchange Rate Models, *Journal of Business and Economic Statistics,* 5, 87-97.

In: Macroeconomics
Editor: Carly M. Hutson
ISBN: 978-1-63463-596-7

Chapter 3

PRODUCTIVITY CHANGE AND EFFICIENCY OF GHANA'S BANKS: APPLICATION OF DATA ENVELOPMENT ANALYSIS AND MALMQUIST PRODUCTIVITY INDEX

***Kofi Adjei-Frimpong*[1], *Christopher Gan*[*2] *and Baiding Hu*[3]**

[1]Research Associate, Faculty of Commerce, Department of Accounting, Economics and Finance, Lincoln University, Canterbury, New Zealand
[2]Professor of Accounting and Finance, Faculty of Commerce, Department of Accounting, Economics and Finance, Lincoln University, Canterbury, New Zealand
[3]Senior Lecturer, Faculty of Commerce, Department of Accounting, Economics and Finance, Lincoln University, Canterbury, New Zealand

ABSTRACT

This study assesses total factor productivity growth (and its components, such as technical efficiency change, technical change, pure technical efficiency change, scale efficiency change) and technical efficiency (and its components, such pure technical efficiency and scale efficiency) in Ghana's banking industry for the period 2002-2010,

[*] Tel: 64-3-325-2811, Fax: 64-3-325-3847, Email: Christopher.Gan@Lincoln.ac.nz.

sub-periods 2002-2006 and 2007-2010 as a result of Ghana's bank deregulation. This paper employs the data envelopment analysis (DEA) method and DEA-based Malmquist total factor productivity index to measure and decompose the overall technical efficiency and total factor productivity growth, respectively. The results suggest that Ghana's banks are technical inefficiency for the period 2002-2010 as well as the sub-periods, which is attributed to both pure technical and scale inefficiency. In addition, the results show total factor productivity grew on average over the period 2002-2010 and sub-period 2002-2006. The improvements in both periods are exclusively driven by technological progress because of deterioration in efficiency change for both periods. However, the findings exhibit the deterioration in total factor productivity for the period 2007-2010 is exclusively the result of the decline in efficiency change. All three periods report a decline in efficiency change due to the deterioration in both pure technical and scale efficiency change. The most remarkable years are 2005/2006 and 2007/2008 where the total factor productivity and its components all improved.

JEL Classifications: E44, E50, G21

Keywords: efficiency, productivity, banks, Ghana

INTRODUCTION

Over the past two decades, Ghana's banking industry has gradually and steadily implemented financial deregulation. The financial reforms were undertaken as part of the structural economic adjustment programme launched in 1983. Before the financial reforms, banks in Ghana were saddled with inefficiency (leading to high operating costs), insufficient capital, inadequate loans loss provisions and huge nonperforming loans and experienced significant political influence (International Monetary Fund, 1999; World Bank, 1989). Most of the banks in Ghana were state-owned and had a monopoly over the banking sector in regard to their operations and were directed to allocate large part of their total loan portfolio to selected sectors in the economy. Hence, the government essentially became the biggest borrower. Ghana's banks' lending decisions were basically directed by the government and were not based on the borrowers' credibility and viability of the project (a pattern also observed by Huang et al.'s (2011) on China's banking sector). As a result of financial reforms, the banking industry of Ghana has modernised its distribution networks, adopted information technology, and provided new banking products and services such as automated teller machines, telephone banking, mobile banking and internet banking. These developments appear to have precipitated changes in the productivity and efficiency of the Ghanaian banking industry. The number of banks in Ghana has also increased from 10 in 1987 (pre-reforms era) to 27 in 2014 after acquisitions (e.g. Intercontinental Bank Ghana by Access Bank, 2012; The Trust Bank by Ecobank, 2012; Amalgamated Bank by Bank of Africa, 2011) and new entry (The Royal Bank, 2011; Energy Bank, 2011). The number of bank branches also increased from 309 in 2002 to 776 in 2010.

The global financial crisis which originated as a result of the recent U.S. subprime mortgage crisis affected many banking systems across the world that negatively affected the world economy. The crisis did not directly affect the banks in Ghana as Ghana banking industry had little or no securitisation which was the source of the U.S. subprime mortgage crisis, but indirectly due to Ghana's economic relation (via trade) with other economies that were affected. This generated credit crunch which affected the lending activities of Ghana's banks. However, banks are gradually easing their credit stance after a decline in loans and advances since 2007. To raise Ghana's banks low capital base, the Bank of Ghana announced in 2008 that all banks increased their minimum capital from GHC7 million (about US$3.5 million) to GHC60 million (about US$30 million) by December 2012. Bank recapitalization policy has recently become a vital part of Ghana's banking industry reforms (Bank of Ghana intends to increase its capital base to GH¢120 million), to avert banking industry crises or failures. Bank of Ghana has twice increased the minimum capital requirement in 2003 and 2009. This recapitalization policy is to increase the capacity of the banks to mobilise additional resources to finance the long-term development needs of the Ghanaian economy in order to accelerate economic growth.

Intuitively, the purpose of bank deregulation is to improve efficiency and productivity through the creation of a more competitive environment leading to increase in investment which stimulates economic growth. Thus, when banks efficiently mobilise and allocate funds, this lowers the cost of capital to firms and accelerates capital accumulation and productivity growth (McKinnon, 1973). However, results of previous empirical studies on bank efficiency and productivity are mixed (Berger & Humprey, 1997).

This paper examines productivity change and technical efficiency in Ghana's banking industry for the period 2002-2010, that covers a significant part of Ghana's financial deregulation and the global financial crisis. The study compares the results of efficiency and productivity change between the sub-periods 2002-2006 financial reforms and 2007-2010 U.S. subprime mortgage crisis. The study employs data envelopment analysis (DEA) and the DEA-based Malmquist productivity index to measure and decompose technical efficiency and total factor productivity change, respectively. The overall technical efficiency is decomposed into pure technical efficiency and scale efficiency, while the productivity change is decomposed into technical change (technological change), technical efficiency change, pure technical efficiency change and scale efficiency change to comprehensive analyse Ghana's banking industry.

This study offers the most updated analysis on bank efficiency and productivity change in Ghana. There is no empirical study conducted on the impact of the global financial crisis on bank efficiency and productivity change in Ghana. Hence, this research attempts to fill the gap in the literature by providing empirical evidence to the existing literature on efficiency and productivity change. The empirical analysis of bank productivity change and efficiency is very important for setting up banking policy measures. Thus, the analysis would help policymakers and bank regulator to ensure efficient bank supervision and regulation changes and bank managers to identify the sources of efficiency and bank productivity change.

The remainder of this paper is organized as follows: Section 2 reviews the literature on bank efficiency and productivity and Section 3 presents the data and methodology, while Section 4 discusses the empirical results. Section 5 provides the summary and conclusions.

LITERATURE REVIEW

Productivity and efficiency studies on the banking industry in developing economies are substantially limited. However, for some years now bank efficiency has been the subject of many studies (see Yildirim, 2002; Das & Ghosh, 2006; Casu & Girardone, 2009; Staub et al., 2010; Sufian & Habibullah, 2010; Adjei-Frimpong et al., 2014) as a result of financial reforms carried out across both developed and developing countries. Yildirim (2002) applies DEA method to estimate technical and scale efficiencies of Turkish commercial banks over the period 1988 to 1999 and find that Turkish banks' inefficiency are mainly due to scale inefficiency which is attributed to decreasing returns to scale. Casu & Girardone (2009), in their study on five European banking sectors, find an increase in input waste from 2000-2001 resulting in lower average efficiencies. The authors further explain that decreases in bank efficiency can be the cause of bank consolidation which allows managers to exploit market power. Das & Ghosh (2006) examine the performance of Indian commercial banks over the period 1992-2002 and report high level of inefficiency of some Indian banks. A recent study by Sufian & Habibullah (2009) assess the effect of the 1997 Asian financial crisis on the efficiency of the Korean banking sector. The authors find a high degree of inefficiency in the Korean banking industry, which was more pronounced in the year after the Asian financial crisis. More recently, Sufian & Habibullah (2010) investigate the efficiency of the Thai banking sector from 1999 to 2008. Their findings show that the inefficiency in the Thai banking sector is the result of the scale inefficiency. On the efficiency of the Brazilian banking industry over the post-privatization period of 2000–2007, Tecles & Tabak (2010) use both Bayesian stochastic frontier and DEA approaches report that large banks are the most efficient banks. In another study on Brazilian banks over the same period 2000–2007, Staub et al. (2010) find that banks in Brazil are inefficient which was attributed mainly to technical inefficiency rather than allocative inefficiency.

In terms of bank productivity change, some previous banking studies attribute productivity growth to technological change, for instance, for the U.S. banks (Mukherjee et al., 2001), European banks (Casu et al., 2004; Koutsomanoli-Filippaki et al., 2009), Kenyan banks (Kamau, 2011), Indian banks (Zhao et al., 2008) and Chinese banks (Matthews et al., 2009; Matthews and Zhang, 2010). On the contrary, others studies have also found efficiency gains, for example, for Norwegian banks (Berg et al., 1992), Korean banks (Gilbert & Wilson, 1998) and Turkish banks (Isik & Hassan, 2003). Berg et al. (1992) study, one of the first studies to assess productivity change, applies the Malmquist index to estimate bank productivity change in Norway during the period 1980–1989. The results show that the improvement in productivity in Norway's banks is due to the improvements in efficiency. Isik & Hassan (2003) investigate the impact of financial reforms embarked in the 1980s on the productivity of Turkish commercial banks and find that considerable increase in banks productivity in Turkey. The gains are assigned to improvements in efficiency. In addition, Koutsomanoli-Filippaki et al. (2009) study on bank efficiency and productivity change across Central and Eastern European countries for the period 1998–2003 indicates that productivity change is driven by technological change rather than efficiency change. Gilbert & Wilson (1998) assess productivity in Korean banks for the period 1980-1994 and find that the period experienced considerable productivity growth. Investigating the effect of deregulation on productivity on Indian commercial banks, Zhao et al. (2008) findings show that the Indian banking industry achieved improvement in productivity, driven by technological progress. More recently, Matthews et al. (2009) investigate the productivity growth of a sample of city commercial banks and the nationwide banks of China. Their findings indicate improvement in productivity growth in the average city commercial banks is attributed to technological progress and efficiency gain. In addition, individual state-owned and joint-stock banks did improve their productivity growth.

On the banking sectors in Africa, Kamau (2011) uses DEA and Malmquist Productivity Index to estimate bank efficiency and productivity in Kenya. The results reveal that the banks in Kenya are not efficient. In addition, the findings show that large banks in Kenya are the most efficient followed by the medium banks. However, the results indicate an improvement in the productivity that is attributed to the technological progress mainly experienced by larger domestic banks and foreign owned banks. Most recently, Maredza & Ikhide (2013) assess the impact of global financial crisis on South Africa's banks efficiency and productivity over the period 2000-2010. Their results find that bank efficiency and productivity in South Africa have declined during the global financial crisis, but generally mild.

Finally, Karanu (2010) examines the productivity and efficiency of Ghana's banking industry for the period 1997-2006 using both DEA and Stochastic Frontier Analysis methods. The author's findings indicate that there is more room for improvement in efficiency for Ghana's banks.

DATA AND METHODOLOGY

Data

The sample data is a balanced panel data of 18 banks with 162 annual observations, which accounts for more than 90% of bank assets in the time period under consideration. The data are based on the balance sheets and income statements of the banks' annual reports obtained from Price-waterhouseCoopers. This investigation spans over the period from 2002 to 2010, and covers important part of the Ghana's banking reforms period, 2002-2006 and the global financial crisis period 2007-2010. The time period 2007-2010 is specifically selected to study the effects of the recent global financial crisis on the efficiency and productivity of Ghana's banks. We employ the

DEA method and DEA-based Malmquist productivity index to measure and decompose technical efficiency and productivity change respectively.

Specification of Input and Output

Following Yildirim (2002), Das & Ghosh (2006), Casu & Girardone (2006), Staub et al. (2010), Sufian & Habibullah (2010) and Moffat & Valadkhani (2011) studies, the specification of input and output variables used in this study is a variation of the intermediation approach originally developed by Sealy & Lindley (1977). The study uses deposits, labour (personnel expenses) and capital expenses as inputs for producing loans and other earning assets. Hence our study specifies three inputs and two outputs that are described in the Table 1.

Table 1. Variables Used in the Study to Compute Bank Efficiency

Variable	Name	Description
Inputs:		
Deposits		Customers deposits
Labour Capital-related expanses		Personnel expenses of bank staff such as salaries, wages and benefits operating expenses minus personnel expenses
Output:		
Loans		Total customers' loans
Other earning assets		Banks' investments in different types of securities (e.g. government securities, bonds, Treasury bill and equity investment)

Table 2 presents the summary statistics of the input and output variables employed in the study. The descriptive statistics are calculated for the total samples. The most vital input resource for banks in Ghana is deposits which are used to execute banking activities such as lending and investment. Labour (personnel expenses) and capital expenses are other input resources used in the production of banking products and services considered in this study. In Ghana, loans and other earning assets are important generator of revenues and account for about two thirds of the bank assets. The banking industry in Ghana relies mostly on interest income. Despite the adoption of universal banking policy, Ghana banks still concentrate on the traditional deposits and lending activities (Adjei-Frimpong et al., 2014). This suggests a lower level of diversification in banks' sources of income in Ghana.

Table 2. Descriptive Statistics for the period 2002-2010

Variable	Minimum	Maximum	Mean	Standard Deviation
Deposits	3,425.14	1,575,281.05	256,607.88	304,361.81
Labour	122.66	84,988.70	13,103.62	16,436.11
Capital-related expanses	41.82	19,961.70	1,925.94	2,528.94
Loans	1,721.61	1,265,516.73	164,882.93	199,838.71
Other earning assets	1,260.15	741,297.00	81,446.42	114,536.20

Notes: Values are in thousands of Ghana Cedis.

DEA Model

The DEA method is used to estimate bank efficiency. DEA is used extensively in studies of the banking industry (see Aly et al., 1990; Chen et al., 1998; Sathye, 2001; Isik & Hassan, 2002; Casu & Girardone, 2006; Ataullah & Le, 2006; Havrylchyk, 2006; Pasiouras et al., 2007; Moffat & Valadkhani, 2011).

The overall technical efficiency (OTE) computed is decomposed into pure technical efficiency (PTE) and scale efficiency (SE). The number of banks in Ghana is small and DEA is particularly suited to working with small sample size. DEA does not specify any functional form of the underlying production relationship (Berger & Humphrey, 1997) and does not take into account random errors. DEA sets up an efficient frontier based on observed best performances and evaluates the efficiency of each decision making unit (DMU) relative to the frontier.

DMUs that lie on the frontier are efficient. Firms that are not on the frontier are inefficient (Das & Ghosh, 2006, 2009). DEA can be implemented by assuming either constant returns to scale (Charnes et al., 1978) or variable returns to scale (Banker et al., 1984).

In this study, the input-oriented DEA model is used to measure the efficiency based on the assumption that managers have more control over inputs than over outputs. The input-oriented technical efficiency of each bank in the sample, under the assumption of constant returns to scale (CRS), is measured as:

$$\text{Minimise}_{\theta,\lambda}\ \theta, \text{subject to} - y_i + Y\lambda \geq 0, \theta x_i - X\lambda \geq 0, \lambda \geq 0 \quad (1)$$

where θ is the overall technical efficiency score, λ is N x 1 is a vector of constants or weights attached to each of the efficient banks, x_i and y_i represent vector of inputs and outputs respectively for the *i*-th bank, and X and Y are the matrix of observed inputs and outputs for all the banks. The DEA formulation can be changed to include variable returns to scale (VRS) by introducing the restriction $N1'\lambda = 1$ as follows (Banker et al., 1984):

$$\text{Minimise}_{\theta,\lambda}\ \theta, \text{subject to} - y_i + Y\lambda \geq 0, \theta x_i - X\lambda \geq 0, NI'\lambda = 1, \lambda \geq 0 \quad (2)$$

where N1 is a N x 1 vector of ones and θ becomes the measure of pure technical efficiency. Thus, VRS offers a measure of pure technical efficiency. Scale efficiency is then measured as the ratio of overall technical efficiency to pure technical efficiency.

The efficiency score ranges between 0 and 1, with $\theta = 1$implying a technical (or scale) efficiency while $\theta < 1$ indicates technical (or scale) inefficiency.

MALMQUIST PRODUCTIVITY INDEX

This paper estimates total factor productivity change over time using the Malmquist productivity index based on a DEA-based programming method suggested by Fare et al. (1994). This approach is widely used in many previous studies such as Berg et al. (1992) for Norwegian banking sector; Fukuyama (1995) for Japanese banking industry; Mukherjee et al. (2001) for US commercial banks; Canhoto & Dermine (2003) for Portugal; Casu et al.(2003) for European banks). In addition, the productivity change is decomposed into technical change and technical efficiency change. The technical efficiency change is then decomposed into pure technical efficiency change and scale efficiency change. The Malmquist productivity index depends on the constant returns to scale and output-based approach. However, the results would not be different from that of the constant returns to scale and input-oriented approach (Coelli, 1996; Thanassoulis, 2001; Yao et al., 2008). The Malmquist productivity index computes the total factor productivity change between two data points by using the ratio of the distances of each data relative to a commom technology. Following Färe et al. (1994), the output oriented Malmquist productivity change index between period *t* and period *t+1* can be expressed as follows:

$$M_0 = \left[\frac{d_0^t(x_0^t, y_0^t)}{d_0^t(x_0^{t+1}, y_0^{t+1})} \text{x} \frac{d_0^{t+1}(x_0^t, y_0^t)}{d_0^{t+1}(x_0^{t+1}, y_0^{t+1})}\right]^{\frac{1}{2}} \tag{3}$$

M_0 in equation (3) measures the productivity of the production points (x^{t+1}, y^{t+1}) relative to production point (x^t, y^t). The index uses period *t* technology and the next period *t+1* technology. A value of M_0 greater than one suggests positive productivity growth from the period *t* to period *t+1* while a value less than one indicates productivity deterioration. However, a value of M_0 equal to zero exhibits no change in productivity from period *t* to period *t+1*. The Malmquist productivity index in equation (3) can be decomposed into technical change and technical efficiency change as follows:

$$\overline{M_0} = \frac{d_0^t(x_0^t, y_0^t)}{d_0^{t+1}(x_0^{t+1}, y_0^{t+1})}\left[\frac{d_0^{t+1}(x_0^t, y_0^t)}{d_0^t(x_0^t, y_0^t)} \text{x} \frac{d_0^{t+1}(x_0^{t+1}, y_0^{t+1})}{d_0^t(x_0^{t+1}, y_0^{t+1})}\right]^{\frac{1}{2}} \tag{4}$$

where the ratio outside the square brackets measures efficiency changes as:

$$\text{Efficiency change} = \frac{d_0^t(x_0^t, y_0^t)}{d_0^{t+1}(x_0^{t+1}, y_0^{t+1})} \tag{5}$$

Equation (5) measures how much closer to the production frontier the operating unit is in period *t+1* compared to period *t*. The two terms in the square bracket of the equation (4) is:

$$\text{Technical change} = \left[\frac{d_0^{t+1}(x_0^t, y_0^t)}{d_0^t(x_0^t, y_0^t)} \text{x} \frac{d_0^{t+1}(x_0^{t+1}, y_0^{t+1})}{d_0^t(x_0^{t+1}, y_0^{t+1})}\right]^{\frac{1}{2}} \tag{6}$$

which captures the change in the production technology as a shift in the production or efficient frontier, while the change in technical efficiency is the result of movements of firms towards or away from the production frontier. This implies that the product of the change in technical efficiency and technological change yields the total factor productivity change.

A value of efficiency change is greater than, less than or equal to one indicates improvement, decrease or no change in technology, respectively. Similarly, a value of technical change is greater than, less than or equal to one indicates improvement, deterioration or no change in efficiency, respectively.

Similarly, technical efficiency change is further decomposed into the product of pure technical efficiency change (due to the VRS assumption) and scale efficiency change (Fare et al. 1994).

$$\text{Pure technical efficiency change} = \frac{d_0^{t+1}(x_0^{t+1}, y_0^{t+1})vrs}{d_0^{t}(x_0^{t}, y_0^{t})vrs} \tag{7}$$

and

$$\text{Scale efficiency change} = \left[\frac{d_0^{t}(x_0^{t}, y_0^{t})vrs}{d_0^{t}(x_0^{t}, y_0^{t})crs} \text{x} \frac{d_0^{t+1}(x_0^{t+1}, y_0^{t+1})crs}{d_0^{t+1}(x_0^{t+1}, y_0^{t+1})vrs}\right]^{\frac{1}{2}} \tag{8}$$

where crs and vrs refer to constant returns to scale and variable returns to scale, respectively.

EMPIRICAL RESULTS

Table 3 presents the mean level of the overall technical efficiency (OTE), pure technical efficiency (PTE) and scale efficiency (SE) for the period 2002-2010 (whole period and for the two sub-periods 2002-2006 and 2006-2010). The results show that the average overall technical efficiency score for the period 2002-2010 is 0.885. In other words, on average, banks could have produced the same amount of outputs with 11.5 percent fewer input resources. There is much waste of valuable resources in Ghana's banking system over the period under study. Similarly, the average values of the pure technical efficiency and scale efficiency for the period 2002-2010 are 0.946 and 0.936, respectively. This implies that the level of pure technical efficiency inefficiency is 5.4 percent and that of scale inefficiency is 6.4 percent. The pure technical inefficiency indicates bad senior management practices in input-usage and management of the loan portfolio.

Table 3. Mean Technical Efficiency for Ghana's Banks (2002-2010)

	OTE	PTE	SE
2002	0.936	0.962	0.973
2003	0.915	0.951	0.962
2004	0.941	0.969	0.971
2005	0.896	0.942	0.951
2006	0.898	0.939	0.956
2007	0.783	0.947	0.827
2008	0.934	0.956	0.977
2009	0.907	0.944	0.961
2010	0.755	0.901	0.838
Mean: 2002-2010	0.885	0.946	0.936
Mean: 2002-2006	0.917	0.953	0.962
Mean: 2007-2010	0.845	0.937	0.902

Notes: OTE, PTE and SE represent overall technical efficiency, pure technical efficiency and scale efficiency.

The underutilization of input resources by banks in Ghana could, in part, be attributed to banks expansion generating higher amount of fixed assets which are yet to produce returns (see Sathye, 2003). The sources of the overall technical inefficiency for the entire period 2002-2010 is both scale inefficiency and pure technical inefficiency. The results of inefficiency reported in this study are consistent with the findings of Yildirim (2002) for Turkish banks, Ataullah & Le (2004) for Indian and Pakistani banks, Staub et al. (2010) for Brazil, Sufian & Habibullah (2010) for Thai banks and Casu & Girardone (2009) for European banks.

In terms of the sub-periods, the average values of the technical efficiency, pure technical efficiency and scale efficiency are 0.917, 0.953 and 0.962 for sub-period 2002-2006 and 0.845, 0.937 and 0.902 for 2007-2010, respectively. Thus, the efficiency scores indicate that Ghana's banks are inefficient. Similar to the period 2002-2010, both scale inefficiency and pure technical inefficiency are the source of the overall technical inefficiency for both sub-periods 2002-2006 and 2007-2010. However, the problem is more of a scale inefficiency than pure technical inefficiency for the entire period 2002-2010 and the sub-period 2007-2010 as pure technical efficiency is higher than the scale efficiency. In other words, Ghana's banks technical inefficiency is the results of improper scale operation. This could be attributed to the increased competition and introduction of technologies of Ghana's banking industry, as part of the banking reforms which could be reasons for Ghana's banks deviation from an optimal scale of operation. In contrast, the period 2002-2006 reveal that scale efficiency is higher than the pure technical efficiency, therefore, the scale inefficiency forms a smaller source of technical inefficiency than pure technical inefficiency for Ghana's banks. This may be due to competition and unprofitable bank branches (due to rapid expansion of branch networks).

In terms of yearly results, the year 2010 shows the lowest mean efficiency for the entire period under study; 0.755 for overall technical efficiency, 0.901 for pure technical efficiency and 0.838 for scale efficiency. The results show remarkable deterioration in the efficiency scores in Ghana's banks for the year 2010. For instance, the average technical efficiency declined substantially from 0.907 in 2009 to 0.755 in 2010, while efficiency scores fell from 0.944 in 2009 to 0.901 in 2010 for pure technical efficiency and from 0.961 in 2009 to 0.838 in 2010 for scale efficiency.

Table 4 presents the Malmquist productivity index (tfpch) results and its components; technical efficiency change (effch), technical change (techch), pure efficiency change (pech) and scale efficiency change (sech), for the entire period (2002-2010) under study and for the two sub-periods 2002-2006 and 2007-2010. The results in Table 4 show a higher Malmquist productivity index, M=1.012, that is, an increase of 0.012 per year during the period 2002-2010 and M=1.054, an increase of 0.054 per year over the period 2002-2006. This implies that bank productivity has increased on average by 1.2 percent per year over the entire period 2002-2010 and 5.4 percent for the sub-period 2002-2006. This improvement in both periods is exclusively driven by technological progress of 4.3 percent for period 2002-2010 and 12.7 percent for period 2002-2006 since there is an average deterioration in efficiency of -3.0 percent per year for period 2002-2010 and -6.5 percent for period 2002-2006. The deterioration in efficiency for the period 2002-2010 is the results of the deterioration in pure technical efficiency of -1 percent and in scale efficiency of -2 percent. Similarly, the negative change in efficiency is the result of pure technical inefficiency of 1.7 percent as well as scale inefficiency of 4.9 percent for the period 2002-2006. These results are indications of bad bank management and inappropriate optimal size.

Table 4. Decomposition of Productivity Change of Ghana's Banks

Year	effch	techch	pech	sech	tfpch
2002/2003	0.979	0.884	0.990	0.988	0.865
2003/2004	1.030	0.830	1.021	1.009	0.855
2004/2005	0.939	1.288	0.967	0.971	1.209
2005/2006	1.009	1.043	1.000	1.009	1.053
2006/2007	0.863	0.919	1.005	0.858	0.792
2007/2008	1.211	1.197	1.012	1.197	1.450
2008/2009	0.967	1.036	0.982	0.985	1.003
2009/2010	0.812	1.251	0.944	0.860	1.015
Mean: 2002-2010	0.970	1.043	0.990	0.980	1.012
Mean: 2002-2006	0.935	1.127	0.983	0.951	1.054
Mean: 2007-2010	0.952	1.047	0.991	0.960	0.996

Notes: effch, techch, pech, sech and tfpch represent technical efficiency change, technical change, pure technical efficiency change, scale efficiency change and total factor productivity change. All indexes are geometric averages.

The findings of productivity growth driven by technological progress is consistent with the findings of the previous studies by Casu et al. (2004) on European banks, Mukherjee et al. (2001) for US banks, Koutsomanoli-Filippaki et al. (2009) for Central and Eastern European banks, Rezitis (2006) for Greek banks, Matthew et al. (2009) for Chinese banks, Kamau (2011) for Kenyan banks and Zhao et al. (2008) for Indian banks. However, the finding is not consistent with the study by Karanu (2010) that exhibits deterioration in the Ghana's banks productivity. For the same period 2007-2010, Ghana's banks still achieved a technological progress of 4.7 percent. The decline in productivity could be results of the cost associated with the introduction of information, increased competition and the effect of the global financial crisis credit crunch that affected lending activities of banks in Ghana. The deterioration in productivity for the 2007-2010 period underscore the view that bank deregulation does not always increase productivity. The findings are consistent with the studies by Humphrey & Pulley (1997) for US banks, Casu et al. (2003) for French and German banks, Maredza & Ikhide (2013) for South African banks and Karanu (2010) for Ghana's banks. The Malmquist productivity index for the sub-period 2002-2006 (average rate of 5.4 percent per year) is higher than the period 2007-2010 (average rate of 0.4 percent per year). This is the result of the increase in bank competition and introduction of technology by Ghana's banks. Undoubtedly, this period observed the introduction of advanced technologies into Ghana's banking industry such as Automatic Teller Machines, electronic funds transfer at point of sale networks, telephone and internet banking.

The most remarkable periods are 2005/2006 and 2007/2008 where the total productivity and its components all improved. The results indicate that, over the period 2005/2006 (2007/2008), the banks in Ghana have improved their productivity by 5.3 percent (45 percent), technology by 4.3 percent (19.7 percent), efficiency 0.9 percent (21.1 percent), pure technical efficiency by zero percent (1.2 percent) and scale efficiency by 0.9 percent (19.7 percent) per year.

These results indicate that the improvement in productivity is driven by technological change (via adoption of new technology, new services and increased competition) and efficiency change (via increased competition and high operating cost). However, the productivity growth in 2008/2009 and 2009/2010 are completely driven by technological progress as efficiency deteriorates.

CONCLUSION

This study applied the DEA method and DEA-based Malmquist productivity index to measure and decompose the overall technical efficiency and total factor productivity change, respectively. These were used to analyse the efficiency and productivity changes in Ghana's banking industry over the period 2002-2010 and the sub-periods 2002-2006 and 2007-2010. The results suggest that Ghana's banks are technical inefficient for the entire period under study as well as sub-periods and it is attributed to both pure technical inefficiency and scale inefficiency. The pure technical inefficiency of Ghana's banks may be due to competition, unprofitable bank branches (due to rapid expansion of branch networks) while the problem of improper scale operation could be attributed to the increased competition and introduction of technologies into Ghana's banking industry.

In terms of total factor productivity, the improvement in total factor productivity of Ghana's banking industry is exclusively driven by technological progress. Ghana's banks are less efficient but increased their productivity due to increase in new technologies. This implies that Ghana's banks improve their information technologies but are unable to make most of the new technologies resulting in technical inefficiency due to bank bad management. In addition, the results of the scale efficiency show that Ghana's banks have deviated from the optimal size. The most remarkable periods are 2005/2006 and 2007/2008 where the total factor productivity and its components all improved, an indication of good bank management and appropriate optimal size. The improvement in productivity is the result of technological change through the adoption of new technology and new services and products, and efficiency change through increased competition and high operating cost. Similarly, the productivity growth in 2008/2009 and 2009/2010 are entirely due to technological progress as efficiency deteriorates.

REFERENCES

Adjei-Frimpong, K., Gan, C., & Hu, B. (2014). Cost efficiency of Ghana's banking industry: A panel data analysis. *The International Journal of Business and Finance Research*, 8(2), 69-86.

Aly, H. Y., Grabowski, R., Pasurka, C., & Rangan, N. (1990). Technical, scale, and allocative efficiencies in U.S. banking: An empirical investigation. *The Review of Economics and Statistics, 72*(2), 211-218.

Ataullah, A., & Le, H. (2006). Economic reforms and bank efficiency in developing countries: the case of the Indian banking industry. *Applied Financial Economics, 16*(9), 653-663.

Bank of Ghana (2008) Bank of Ghana Raises Minimum Capital Requirements for Banks, *Bank of Ghana Press Release,* February 14, Accra.

Banker, R.D., Charnes, A. & Cooper, W.W. (1984), Some Models for Estimating Technical and Scale Inefficiencies in Data Envelopment Analysis, *Management Science* 30 (9), 1078-1092.

Berg, S.A., Førsund, F.R., & Jansen, E.S., (1992). Malmquist indices of productivity growth during the deregulation of Norwegian banking, 1980–1989. *Scandinavian Journal of Economics* 94, 211–228.

Berger, A. N., & Humphrey, D. B. (1997). Efficiency of financial institutions: International survey and directions for future research. *European Journal of Operational Research, 98*(2), 175-212.

Canhoto, A, & Dermine, J (2003), A note on banking efficiency in Portugal, new vs.old banks, *Journal of Banking & Finance* 27: 2087-2098.

Casu, B., Girardone, C., & Molyneux, P., (2004). Productivity change in European banking: a comparison of parametric and non-parametric approaches. *Journal of Banking and Finance* 28, 2521–2540.

Casu, B., & Girardone, C., (2006). Bank competition, concentration and efficiency in the single European market. *The Manchester School, 74*(4), 441-468.

Casu, B., & Girardone, C., (2009). Testing the relationship between competition and efficiency in banking: A panel data analysis. *Economics Letters, 105*(1), 134137.

Charnes, A., Cooper, W.W., Rhodes, E., (1978). Measuring the efficiency of decision making units, *European Journal of Operational Research* 2, 429-44.

Chen, T., & Yeh, T. L. (1998). A Study of efficiency evaluation in Taiwan's banks. *International Journal of Service Industry Management, 9*(5), 402-415.

Coelli, Tim (1996), A guide to DEAP version 2.1: A data envelopment analysis (computer) program, Working Paper 96/08, Centre for Efficiency and Productivity Analysis.

Das, A., & Ghosh, S. (2006). Financial deregulation and efficiency: An empirical analysis of Indian banks during the post reform period. *Review of Financial Economics 15*, 193-221.

Das, A., & Ghosh, S. (2009). Financial deregulation and profit efficiency: A nonparametric analysis of Indian banks. *Journal of Economics and Business, 61*(6), 509-528.

Fare, R, Shawna, G, & Lovell, C.A.K (1994), *Production Frontiers*, Cambridge University Press.

Farrell, M. J. (1957). The measurement of productive efficiency, *Journal of the Royal Statistical Society*, *Series A* 120(3), 253-282.

Fukuyama, H (1995). Measuring efficiency and productivity growth in Japanese banking: A non-parametric approach, *Applied Financial Economics* 5: 95-117.

Gilbert, R. A., & Wilson, P. W. (1998). Effects of deregulation on the productivity of Korean banks. *Journal of Economics and Business, 50*(2), 133-155.

Havrylchyk, O. (2006). Efficiency of the Polish banking industry: Foreign versus domestic banks. *Journal of Banking & Finance, 30*(7), 1975-1996.

Huang, T., Chiang, L., & Chen, K.(2011). An empirical study of bank efficiencies and technology gaps in European banking. *The Manchester School, 79(4)* 839-860.

International Monetary Fund. (1999). Ghana: Selected issues. *IMF Staff Country Report No.99/3*, International Monetary Fund, Washington, D.C.

Isik, I., & Hassan, M. K. (2002). Technical, scale and allocative efficiencies of Turkish banking industry. *Journal of Banking & Finance, 26*(4), 719-766.

Isik, I., & Hassan, M. K., (2003). Financial deregulation and total factor productivity change: an empirical study of Turkish commercial banks, *Journal of Banking and Finance* 27, 1455-1485.

Kamau, A. W. (2011). Intermediation efficiency and productivity of the banking sector in Kenya. *Interdisciplinary Journal of Research in Business*, 1(9), 12-26

Karanu, S (2010). Productivity and Efficiency in the Ghanaian Banking Sector (Using DEA and SFA). Working paper series (papers.ssrn.com)

Koutsomanoli-Filippaki, A., Margaritis, D., & Staikouras, C., (2009). Efficiency and productivity growth in the banking industry of Central and Eastern Europe. *Journal of Banking and Finance* 33, 557–567.

Malmquist, S., (1953). Index numbers and indifference surfaces, *Trabajos de Estatistica*, 4, 209-242.

Maredza, A & Ikhide, S (2013). Measuring the Impact of the Global Financial Crisis on Efficiency and Productivity of the Banking System in South Africa. *Mediterranean Journal of Social Sciences,* 4(6).

Matthews, K., & Zhang, N., (2010). Bank productivity in China 1997–2007: measurement and convergence. *China Economic Review* 21, 617–628.

Matthews, K., Zhang, X., Guo, J., (2009). Nonperforming loans and productivity in Chinese Banks, 1997–2006. *Chinese Economy* 42, 30–47.

McKinnon, R. I., (1973). *Money and Capital in Economic Development.* The Brookings Institution, Washington, DC.

Moffat, B. D., & Valadkhani, A. (2011). Efficiency of Botswana's financial institutions: A data envelopment analysis. *Applied Economics Letters, 18*(7), 697-702.

Mukherjee, K., Ray, S.C., Miller, S.M (2001). Productivity growth in large US commercial banks: the initial post-deregulation experience, *Journal of Banking and Finance* 25, 913-939.

Pasiouras, F., Sifodaskalakis, E., & Zopounidis, C. (2007). Estimating and analysing the cost efficiency of Greek cooperative banks: an application of two-stage data envelopment analysis. *Working Paper, School of Management,* University of Bath, available at: http://www.bath.ac.uk/ management/research/papers.html

PricewaterhouseCoopers. (2006). *Ghana Banking Survey*. Accra.

PricewaterhouseCoopers. (2009). *Ghana Banking Survey*. Accra.

PricewaterhouseCoopers. (2011). *Ghana Banking Survey*. Accra.

PricewaterhouseCoopers. (2012). *Ghana Banking Survey*. Accra.

Rezitis, A.N., (2006). Productivity growth in the Greek banking industry: a non-parametric approach *Journal of Applied Economics.* 9(1), 119-138.

Sathye, M. (2001). X-efficiency in Australian banking: An empirical investigation. *Journal of Banking & Finance, 25*(3), 613-630.

Sathye, M. (2003). Efficiency of banks in a developing economy: The case of India. *European Journal of Operational Research, 148(3), 662-671.*

Sealey, G.W., and Lindley, J.T., (1977). Inputs, outputs and a theory of production and cost at depository financial institutions. *Journal of Finance* 32, 1251-1266.

Staub, R. B., da Silva e Souza, G., and Tabak, B. M. (2010). Evolution of bank efficiency in Brazil: A DEA approach. *European Journal of Operational Research, 202*(1), 204-213.

Sufian, F. (2009), Determinants of bank efficiency during unstable macroeconomic environment: empirical evidence from Malaysia, *Research in International Business and Finance* 23 (1), 54-77.

Sufian, F., & Habibullah, M. S. (2010). Bank-specific, industry-specific and macroeconomic determinants of bank efficiency: Empirical evidence from the Thai banking sector. *Margin: The Journal of Applied Economic Research, 4*(4), 427–461.

Thanassoulis, E. (2001). Introduction to the theory and application of Data Envelopment Analysis, (Kluwer Academic Publishers, Boston).

Tecles, P. L., & Tabak, B. M. (2010). Determinants of bank efficiency: The case of Brazil. *European Journal of Operational Research, 207*(3), 1587-1598.

World Bank. (1989). Ghana: Structural adjustment for growth. Report No. 7515-GH, World Bank, Washington, DC.

Yao, S., Han, Z. and Feng, G. (2008). Ownership Reform, Foreign Competition and Efficiency of Chinese Commercial Banks: A Non-parametric Approach, *The World Economy*, 31(10), 1310–1326.

Yildirim, C. (2002). Evolution of banking efficiency within an unstable macroeconomic environment: the case of Turkish commercial banks. *Applied Economics, 34*(18), 2289-2301).

Zhao, T., Casu, B., Ferrari, A., (2008). Deregulation and productivity growth: a study of Indian commercial banking, *International Journal of Business Performance Management*, 10(4), 318 - 343.

INDEX

O

P

R

S

T

U

V

W

Y